Walter White

Rhymes

Walter White

Rhymes

ISBN/EAN: 9783337424480

Printed in Europe, USA, Canada, Australia, Japan

Cover: Foto ©Thomas Meinert / pixelio.de

More available books at **www.hansebooks.com**

RHYMES.

BY WALTER WHITE.

BY THE SAME AUTHOR.

To Switzerland and Back.

A Londoner's Walk to the Land's End, and a Trip to the Scilly Isles. Second Edition.

On Foot through Tyrol.

A July Holiday in Saxony, Bohemia, and Silesia.

A Month in Yorkshire. Fourth Edition.

Northumberland and the Border.

All Round the Wrekin.

Eastern England, from the Thames to the Humber. 2 vols.

Contents.

	PAGE
My Books	1
To a Grasshopper	4
The Electric Telegraph	6
"Those Eighteen"	9
The Beechen Woods	11
A Birthday Rhyme	13
Sonnets :—	
Cloud and Light	14
Waifs of Beauty	14
"Daniel"	15
The Enemy	15
The Veil	16
The Albatross	17
Words	19
Ballads :—	
The Luck of Edenhall	21
The Sisters of Beverley	25
Towton Field (a Fragment)	28
The Tree	29
The Battle of Beth-Horon	31
Hope for all	33
The Hills	35
A Marriage-Day Rhyme	39
Silchester (Calleva Romanorum)	41
Work or Rest	45
To Adversity	47

	PAGE
Aspiration	49
The Elves—a Day Dream	51
Eighteen-hundred and fifty-one	61
Erebus and Terror	75
William Tell, a Poem for Children	84
Das Lied von Paneveggio	124
Speckbacher and his little Son (Translated from Seidl's Speckbacher und sein Söhnlein)	127
A Wedding-Breakfast Speech	129

FOREWORD.

Whoso looks on life but sees
Life is full of cadences?
If to-day we feel a sorrow,
And a gladness on the morrow,
We are not to think it plain
Sorrow will not come again ;
Or that gladness will endure
All our grievances to cure :
Soon or later each returns,
Bearing roses—funeral urns.

Thus with cadence come and go
All our moods of joy and woe.

Here, rehearsing certain fancies,
Born of varied circumstances,
Linking life's strong, youthful day
With years that see the hair turn gray :
Cadences of hope and fear,
Real or hollow, dark or clear,
From divers places, divers climes—
I have shaped them into RHYMES.

RHYMES.

MY BOOKS.

My benison upon ye, Books,—
Upon your ever-constant looks!
Still the same seems every tome
To welcome me when I come home.

Now from daily task releast,
I can hold my nightly feast;
With philosophers discourse,
Wonder at polemics hoarse;
Feed on rhyme or flirt with rumour
As may best befit my humour.

Blessed comforters are ye,
Well-springs of serenity,—
Curing all sad perturbations
With your silent inspirations.
Bitter thought ye soothe, I wis,
Leading where the sweetness is;
When the soul is running riot,
Ye restore her with your quiet;
Or from brooding sorrow wean,
Scene revealing after scene—

RHYMES.

Pointing upward to the Holy,
Guiding downward to the Lowly,
Drawing onward to the Right,
Love inspiring—or delight—
As I turn your varied pages
Stamped with brain-work of the ages.

Oh! how sweet when I come home
To see around me many a tome;
Here to revel, there to muse,
Glean or wander as I chuse.
One or two—so seems to me—
Throb with echoes from the sea;
And in some my sense perceives
The harmony of forest leaves;
Here is one—a bosom book—
That babbles like a mountain brook;
Another yet is gorgeous, still,
As sunset on a distant hill.
Endless landscapes cross my room,
Fancy-decked in twilight gloom;
Autumn, Winter, Summer, Spring,
Wizard books, ye changeful bring!
Something apt for each emotion,
Love, or gladness, or devotion:
Ye to me, instead of wife,
Instead of child—are second life.

Ye at will give up your knowledge
Such as may befit a college,
Tortured into rigid rules,
Vexed with learning of the schools:
Or ye proffer information
With an easy salutation,
As tho' meant, with purpose sly,
To put one off till by-and-by,
And leave me, after all endeavour,
In doubt of what is wise or clever.

Some of ye are as a stream
In whose depths rare jewels gleam :
Happy he who kneels to drink
Leaning o'er the steepy brink,
Catching through the current's flow
Flashes from the gems below.

Admonishers of strife and folly,
Cheerers of black melancholy,
Gentle, most persuasive Teachers,
Or authoritative Preachers ;
Companions full of life and spirit,
Mentors who some grudge inherit ;
Sometimes full of queerest fancies,
Vague as jack-o'-lantern dances :—
Other while ye are as prim
As Quakers neat, sedate and trim.
Three or four are jolly fellows
Whom Time fortifies and mellows ;
Some make pretensions to be witty,
Others chant a stirring ditty :
Suiting every time and season
With a rhyme or with a reason.

Books beloved, ye are to me
An unretorting family :
Ye for each day's irritation
Always bring a compensation.
How shall sadness come or gloom
While ye lie about my room,
Looking down from friendly nooks ?
My benison upon ye, Books !

TO A GRASSHOPPER.

BLITHE frisker in the summer grass
With voice that rings of sounding brass,
Art thou aware thy life will pass
    Ere thou grow'st old?
I watch thy leaps, and say, Alas!
    Thou'lt die of cold.

Machine art thou, or hast thou thought?
By what schoolmaster wert thou taught?
And what experience hast thou bought
    In all thy jumps?
Have they instead of pleasure brought
    But knocks and thumps?

A fife, a trumpet, or a rattle—
Canst tune thy note for dance or battle,
For warning, or for scraps of tattle,
    At thy sweet pleasure?
Thou mightest preach, or soothly prattle,
    If thou hadst leisure.

Small time hast thou to tell the news,
To foster friendship, prove thy views,
For thou it seems must always use—
    Whate'er thy wishes—
A jerky life, like kangaroos,
    Or flying fishes.

At times when on the hill I sit,
And see thy swarming brethren flit,
They seem unto my puzzled wit
    Not melancholic;
But all of solid sunshine knit,
    And ripe for frolic.

Heard all along the rows of hay,
Their notes seem only glad and gay,
While they with leaps amazing play
          O'er field and flow'r;
Enjoying most the hottest day,
          And noontide hour.

Among ye are there high and low?
Are young cicadas trained to go,
And in examinations show
          Of lore a heap?
Or who the loudest trumpet blow,
          Or farthest leap?

Hast duty set before thy life?
Is thy shrill note with anger rife
To keep in awe a pouting wife
          Who seeks to quarrel,
Ready alike for taunt or strife
          About apparel?

Thou'rt quaint enough to be antique,
By Nature shaped in her first week
Of snips of grass by way of freak
          Brown, yellow, green;
And bid through hollow stalks to shriek
          Yet nothing mean.

I fain would think thy life is light,
It lasts but while the sun is bright:
If I thy epitaph indite
          Would this be proper
Here lies till Nature him requite
          A brief grasshopper?

THE ELECTRIC TELEGRAPH.

Hark! the warning needles click,
Hither—thither clear and quick,
Swinging lightly to and fro,
Tidings from afar they show,
While the patient watcher reads
As the rapid movement leads.
He who guides their speaking play
Stands a thousand miles away.
    Sing who will of Orphean lyre,
    Ours the wonder-working wire!

Eloquent, though all unheard,
Swiftly speeds the secret word,
Light or dark, or foul or fair,
Still a message prompt to bear:
None can read it on the way,
None its unseen transit stay.
Now it comes in sentence brief,
Now it tells of loss and grief,
Now of sorrow, now of mirth,
Now a wedding, now a birth,
Now of cunning, now of crime,
Now of trade in wane or prime,
Now of safe or sunken ships,
Now the murderer outstrips,
Now it warns of failing breath,
Strikes or stays the stroke of death.
    Sing who will of Orphean lyre,
    Ours the wonder-working wire!

Now what stirring news it brings,
Plots of emperors and kings;
Or of people grown to strength
Rising from their knees at length:

These to win a state—or school ;
Those for flight or stronger rule.
All that nations dare or feel,
All that serves the commonweal,
All that tells of government,
On the wondrous impulse sent,
Marks how bold Invention's flight
Makes the widest realms unite.
It can fetters break or bind,
Foster or betray the mind,
Urge to war, incite to peace,
Toil impel, bid labour cease.
  Sing who will of Orphean lyre,
  Ours the wonder-working wire !

Speak the word, and think the thought,
Quick 'tis as with lightning caught.
Over—under—lands or seas,
To the far antipodes.
Now o'er cities thronged with men,
Forest now or lonely glen ;
Now where busy Commerce broods,
Now in wildest solitudes ;
Now where Christian temples stand,
Now afar in Pagan land.
Here again as soon as gone,
Making all the earth as one.
Moscow speaks at twelve o'clock,
London reads ere noon the shock ;
Seems it not a feat sublime,
Intellect hath conquered Time !
  Sing who will of Orphean lyre,
  Ours the wonder-working wire !

Flash all ignorance away,
Knowledge seeks for freest play ;
Flash sincerity of speech,
Noblest aims to all who teach ;

Flash till bigotry be dumb,
Deed instead of doctrine come;
Flash to all who truly strive,
Hopes that keep the heart alive;
Flash real sentiments of worth,
Merit claims to rank with Birth;
Flash till Power shall learn the Right,
Flash till Reason conquer Might;
Flash resolve to every mind,
Manhood flash to all mankind.
    Sing who will of Orphean lyre,
    Ours the wonder-working wire!

"THOSE EIGHTEEN."

O! thou whose faith is self-conceit,
Whose righteousness is inward pride,
Whose joy to think thyself as saved,
Though doomed be all the world beside :—
    Of those eighteen bethink thee well
    On whom Siloam's tower fell.

And thou who looking from afar,
Where crime, and woe, and hunger haunt,
Canst see but sinners paid by sin,
And pray thy prayer with easy vaunt :—
    Of those eighteen bethink thee well
    On whom Siloam's tower fell.

And thou whose life appeareth fair,
Whose conduct men unite to praise,
And stumbling lives with thine compare,
And find example in thy ways :—
    Of those eighteen bethink thee well
    On whom Siloam's tower fell.

And thou who in thy daily task
Lett'st duty sleep, while purblind self
Mistakes for light of nobleness
The glitter of increasing pelf :
    Of those eighteen bethink thee well
    On whom Siloam's tower fell.

And thou whose Sabbath days are spent
In proving all thy darling whims,
By darkening the Scripture text,
By singing of polemic hymns :—
    Of those eighteen bethink thee well
    On whom Siloam's tower fell.

And thou who thinkest virtue naught,
Unless repaid by Fortune's gear;
Whose aspiration after Heaven
Springs only from a mortal fear:—
    Of those eighteen bethink thee well
    On whom Siloam's tower fell.

And thou who seest the guiding Hand
In whatsoe'er befits thy choice;
Who fearest more the blame of man
Than whisper of the still, small voice:—
    Of those eighteen bethink thee well
    On whom Siloam's tower fell.

THE BEECHEN WOODS.

The beechen woods, the beechen woods,
   How pleasantly they sound,
While blows the free and gladsome breeze
   Within their green profound :
Now toying with the fallen leaves
   In nooks retired and cool,
Now tracing feathery ripples on
   The darkly shaded pool.

Anon with sudden sweep among
   The topmost branches high,
With the wild maze of shining leaves
   It playeth noisily.
And ever as the arching boughs
   Their flexile arms entwine,
Down through the rustling canopy
   The flickering sunbeams shine,

Bright-flashing here, swift-glancing there,
   The leafy aisles along—
A thousand lights ; the merry breeze
   Gives to the woods a tongue
That tells of beauties manifold,
   And unrestricted good :
What lessons may the thoughtful heart
   Learn in the beechen wood !

Amid the smooth and taper stems,
   As graceful columns tall,
Winds the dim path invitingly,
   With many a rise and fall ;
And glimpses come of harvest fields,
   And tilth, and rural toil,
Where busy reapers bear away
   The bounty of the soil.

RHYMES.

And from the brow far spreads the view,
  O'er the broad vale of Thames
A fair expanse, that well may vie
  With scenes of famous names,
Upland on upland stretching far,
  With quiet dales between,
The river flowing here and there
  Through meadows gay and green.

I've wandered far, seen princely halls,
  And many a ruin'd tower,
Broad lakes, climb'd mountain heights, and sat
  Where trees lone glens embower :
Each passing mile brought fresher thought,
  And many changeful moods,
But none more welcome than I find
  In Berkshire's beechen woods.

A BIRTHDAY RHYME.

Happy days, that bring no fears
Of the growing tale of years!
Days that view, without despair,
Signs of silver in the hair;
When, retiring from the face,
Sprightly charms and youthful grace
Heighten all the charms within,
And our lasting homage win.

Happy days, when we can say,
Every one is holiday!
Not so playful as of yore—
Quiet woos us more and more;
When, if voices ring less clear,
Mellow are they, and sincere:
When among our friends we fare,
Meeting welcome everywhere;
When the little children find
Ways to exorcise our mind,
Coaxing till we ply our tongue
With tales we told when we were young.
Do we then build, without intent,
In living hearts our monument?

When the passions lie asleep,
When the virtues vigils keep,
When experience hath brought
Knowledge with sweet patience fraught,
Such as all our fear allays—
Then we live in happy days!

CLOUD AND LIGHT.

A CLOUD of care had come across my mind ;
Ill-balanced hung the world : here pleasure all ;
There hopeless toil, and cruel pangs that fall
On Poverty, to which but Death seemed kind.
And so, with heart perplex'd, I left behind
The crowd of men, the towns with smoky pall,
And sought the hills, and breathed the mountain wind.
Hath God forgotten, then, the mean and small ?
I mused, and gazed o'er purple fells outroll'd ;
When lo ! beneath an old thatched roof, a gleam
That kindled soon with sunset's gorgeous gold—
Broad panes nor fretted oriel brighter beam.
If glories thus on lattice rude unfold,
Of life unlit by Heaven we may not deem.

WAIFS OF BEAUTY.

As one who walks where mighty kings have trod,
And overcome by greatness more and more,
I pace the tawny sands along the shore
Where ocean dances up to kiss the sod :
And though at times with weary foot I plod
My strength returns when as with foam and roar
And swift as when the Prophet stretched his rod
He flings o'er rock and sand his briny store :
Then waifs of beauty every hour I find,
Now shells, now gems, now flow'rs that walk and breathe,
Now weeds so bright of hue, so deftly twined
That art in vain would seek the like to wreathe :
If such the treasures of his shallow waves
What wonders hides he in his deepest caves !

"DANIEL."

(Royal Academy, 1872).

Why hold they back the lions fierce and grim,
Huddling bewildered on the sandy floor
Where bones bestrew, and ghastly stains of gore—
Why hold they back within that dungeon dim,
Their eyes aflame, jaws wide with hideous roar?
Before them waits their prey. Why spare they him —
A man, with hands fast bound, of aspect hoar,
Why leap they not and tear him limb from limb?
Assyria's mystic symbols mark the wall,
Him to the beasts hath doomed Assyria's king;
Death's stole he wears who erst wore lordly pall;
Why hold the lions back in dread to spring?
A chosen Prophet he, of Hebrew race,
And God, the Living God, looks from his face.

THE ENEMY?

When of the hour men question in their talk,
They say 'How goes the enemy?' and treat
Him of the forelock thus with vain conceit,
While to and fro in mart or mall they walk.
As if he of the swift and silent feet,
Who cometh vain desires and schemes to baulk,
To ripen or destroy, as seemeth meet,
Who shameth error, mocks the boaster's talk,
Were but a foe. Lo! when he pulleth down
For better makes he room: and evermore
He bringeth solace, wisdom, sure renown,
And throws a spell o'er all that went before:
So, in discourse, when drawing near their end
Shall men not rather say 'How goes the friend?'

THE VEIL.

I would not if I could the veil
　From off my future lift,
Or catch a glimpse of coming days
　As thro' a cloudy rift.

Why should I banish from my life
　The pleasure of surprise,
Or baulk the rough vicissitudes
　Which warn and make us wise?

And why count up the toils and snares
　That round my path are set,
As one who tired of watchfulness
　Hopes nothing—waiting yet?

Far better seems it me to live
　With something yet to know,
And up to whatsoe'er befalls,
　Firm fix'd in patience grow.

Then looking back along my life,
　Across its boon and bale,
I see reversed how Time and Will
　Have for me raised the veil.

THE ALBATROSS.

Now upon Australian seas,
Wafted by the tropic breeze,
We salute the Southern Cross,
Seek the swift-winged albatross.
Gulls and petrels scream and play
On the ripple, in the spray ;
At our prow the waters writhe,
Swiftly sails our ship and blithe.

But the albatross appears,
Omen of a tale of fears,
Holding us as with a spell
While we watch him long and well :
Circling round in orbits vast,
Pausing now above the mast,
Laving now his snowy breast
Where the billows sleeping rest.

Now he skims the surface o'er,
Rising, falling evermore :
Floating high on stillest wing,
Now he seems a guardian thing :
Now a messenger of wrath,
Hurrying down his airy path ;
Bearing o'er the liquid plain
Warning of the hurricane.

O ! thou wild and wondrous bird,
Viewing thee, my thought is stirr'd :
Round and round the world thou goest,
And of solitudes thou trowest—
Into trackless wastes hast flown
Which no eye save thine hath known :
Ever tireless—day or night ;
Calm or tempest—ceaseless flight.

Albatross! I envy thee
Oft thy soaring pinions free;
For we deem the realms of air
Too ethereal for care.
Gladness as of endless springs
Seems to me is born with wings.
Thou canst rise and see the sun,
When his course to us is done:
A moral here may us engross,
Thou the teacher—Albatross!

WORDS.

What are words but little sprites,
That flit the world about,—
Stealing every thinker's thought,
And fitful fancy out ;
Shaping every wild conceit,
And prejudice, and doubt ?

Stately, sprightly, solemn, gay,
Thousand shapes they wear,—
Graceful, grim, uncouth, sedate,
From lip to lip they fare,—
Swift harbingers of Joy and Hope,
Or heralds of Despair.

Round about the world they go,
Seeking where to dwell ;
Frolicking in Echo's haunts,
Hiding in a shell ;
Floating sometimes on the wave
From the passing bell.

Law imprisons many a one
In her parchments old ;
Priestcraft tortures until they
A double sense unfold ;
Tyrants and traitors mangle them,
And misers too—for gold.

Blindly in the sophist's net
Hosts all heedless run ;
Wit entraps as many more,—
Martyrs them in fun ;
Music with seductive sound
Melteth them in one.

Scribes there are who bid the sprites
In their cause engage,
Fenced about all cunningly
On a printed page,—
Messengers of good or ill
To every coming age.

Rainbow-wing'd, in sunny light,
From maiden's lip they glide;
Laden, from the lover's heart,
Like honey-bees they slide;
Strong and stern, they bear aloft
Philosophy in pride.

From the Poet's pen they flash,
Lightning-like and strange;
Through the world of human hearts
With him, too, they range:
What he sees and thinks, they keep
Evermore from change.

Round the Prophet of the True
Soar they, shapes of good;
Chasing dismal mists that shroud
Life's deep inner flood;
Shewing it e'er pouring down,
Glory-lit from God.

Representatives of thought,
Essence of the ideal—
Oft, O Words! your majesty,
Your power sublime we feel—
Leading man through purity
Upwards to the Real.

THE LUCK OF EDENHALL.

'TWAS summer-tide when days are long,
　　And holm and haugh are green,
And the mavis sings in the good green wood,
　　And chatters the jay between.

"O, whither dost run thou little foot-page,
　　As swift as hawk on wing?"
"For life—for life to Penrith town
　　I run the leech to bring."

"And wherefore seekest thou the leech?
　　Now up and tell to me."
"O! hold me not, thou weird woman,
　　There's glamour in thine ee."

Oh! there was glamour in her ee;
　　He could not choose but tell:
"My mistress lieth in deadly swoon,
　　The ladye Isabel."

"Now run, now run, thou little foot-page,
　　Run swift as hawk on wing;
But if the leech to succour fail,
　　Then seek the fairies' spring."

The little foot-page hath gone and come,
　　So nimble of foot was he;
And his bonnie bright een were wet with tears,
　　For he loved his dear ladye.

The leech he rode to Edenhall,
　　The while uprose the moon:
But vain his simples and his craft
　　To loose the deadly swoon.

The little foot-page he wept full sore
   And he fell on his knee and he prayed:
He prayed a prayer to Mary Mother,
   And Saint Cuthbert to aid.

His dear ladye hath nurtured him
   Since rose his infant wail,
That night his father's hut was burnt
   By thieves from Liddelsdale.

Then thought he of that weird woman,
   But, Oh! 'tis a fearsome thing
To go at night, in the wan moonlight,
   And walk by the fairies' spring.

Yet will he forth, whate'er betide,
   Yet will he forth and see;
For whom shall he love on earth beside,
   If not his dear ladye?

So softly crept he down the stair,
   And out by the secret door;
And he was aware of a strange music,
   He never had heard before.

And slowly went he o'er the mead,
   And heard the selfsame sound;
And there he saw a companye
   A-dancing round and round.

He fell on his knee behind a bush,
   And his heart beat quick for fear,
Whenever he saw the dainty folk
   Come dancing him a-near.

So beautiful their faces shone,
   So bright their silken sheen;
He could but dread to look thereon,
   And yet he looked, I ween.

BALLADS.

Oh! merrily did they laugh and dance,
    Still tripping round and round ;
But not a blade of grass did bend,
    No flower sunk on the ground.

And ever the music rang full sweet,
    Yet sat no players there ;
It was as if the trees did sing,
    While tinkled harps in air.

Anon they pause, and a crystal cup
    Is dipped in the bubbling spring,
And gliding goes, from lip to lip,
    All round the fairy ring.

And ever it dips and fills again,
    And while the revellers drink,
The brimming water falls like pearls
    Down from the sparkling brink.

But the fay that bears that cup around,
    No mortal eye may see,
"Oh, could my ladye drain that cup!"
    Thought the little foot-page on knee.

Scarce had he thought than to him glides
    The cup from the bubbling spring ;
Him passed before, yet who it bore
    Did nought of shadow fling.

He trembled sore, but he took the cup,
    For the sake of his dear ladye ;
And fast the drops ran down like pearls,
    As he rose up from knee.

And at his feet upon the grass,
    A written scroll was thrown :
Then all at once the music ceased,
    And the fairy folk were gone.

He took the scroll, and he took the cup,
　　Them to the hall he bore;
Then drank the Lady Isabel,
　　And her deadly swoon was o'er.

And the little foot-page he brought the scroll,
　　And shewed it to his lord;
Sir Ralph he looked thereon and read,
　　In olden style, the word—

　　　　'Yf that cuppe
　　　　　Shal breake or fall,
　　　　Farewel the Lucke
　　　　　Of Edenhalle.'

Sir Ralph de Musgrave made a feast,
　　For joy over his ladye;
The little foot-page he stood by her chair,
　　And blithest of all was he.

Sir Ralph de Musgrave built a church,
　　In sweet Saint Cuthbert's prayse,
That men might know whence came the Lucke,
　　And think thereon alwayes.

THE SISTERS OF BEVERLEY.

Upon the eve of Christen-masse—
　Come list ye while I sing,
At Beverley in Holderness
　Befell a wondrous thing.

Sweet sang the abbess and all her nuns,
　And then they knelt on knee,
And prayed unto the blessed Mother
　Of Him who died on tree.

The grief that sweet Saint Mary drede,
　Grieved all in that chapelle;
Then went they forth each one to pray
　Alone in nunrye cell.

Save two fair sisters ling'ring there,
　Sad kneeling on the floor;
Till slowly went they hand in hand,—
　But no man saw them more.

Two sisters tolde for holy life:
　Oh! whither had they fled?
And the abbess wept with all her nuns;
　For lost were they or dead.

Anon the snow set on to melt,
　The sun to shine in Spring,
And flowers to bud, and cuckoo pipe,
　And merry birds to sing.

And Spring danced by, and crowned with boughs,
　Drew lusty Summer on;
And bells were rung when came the eve—
　The eve of good Saint John.

But where bide they, the sisters twain?
  Have the holy sisters fled?
And the abbess and all her nuns bewail'd
  The sisters twain as dead.

Then pace they forth in the eventide,
  In the cool and dusky hour;
And the abbess goes up the stair of stone,
  High on the belfry tower.

Now Christ thee save! thou sweet ladye,
  For on the roof-tree there—
Like as in winsome trance y-rapt,
  She sees the sisters fair.

"Whence come ye, daughters? long astray;"
  "Nay, scarce an hour," they tell
"Since sang we in the Christen-masse,
  And heard the vesper bell."

"Nay, daughters! that was months agone:"
  "Sweet mother an hour we ween;
But we have been in heaven each one,
  And holy angels seen."

What town in all our land is like
  The town of Beverley?
There pilgrims at Saint John his shrine
  Full many wonders see.

Once more the abbess and all her nuns
  Within the chapel meet;
And while they sang the sisters knelt
  Down at the abbess' feet.

Them wolde she kiss, and eke wolde bless,
  And, "Go in peace!" she said:
The sisters, like two lilies pale,
  Sank on the pavement dead.

Eftsoons all sweetly chimed the bells—
  No mortal hand them strake:
So sweet a chime the bells in heaven,
  When rung by angels make.

And when the sisters lay in tomb,
  No change did them betide;
Years long their faces shone as fair
  As on the day they died.

And pilgrims came from all the land,
  And far from over-sea,
To pray at the shrine of the sisters twain,
  And Saint John of Beverley.

TOWTON FIELD.

(A Fragment.)

Palm Sunday chimes were chiming
    All gladsome thro' the air,
And village churls and maidens,
    Knelt in the church at pray'r;
When the Red Rose and the White Rose
    In furious battle reel'd;
And yeomen fought like barons,
    And barons died ere yield.
When mingling with the snow-storm,
    The storm of arrows flew;
And York against proud Lancaster
    His ranks of spearmen threw.
When thunder-like the uproar
    Out-roll'd from either side,
As hand to hand they battled
    From morn to eventide.
When the river ran all gory,
    And in hillocks lay the dead,
And seven and thirty thousand
    Fell for the White and Red.

   *   *   *   *

When o'er the bar of Micklegate,
    They changed each ghastly head;
Set Lancaster upon the spikes
    Where York had bleached and bled.

   *   *   *   *

There still wild roses growing,
    Frail tokens of the fray,—
And the hedgerow green bear witness,
    Of Towton field that day.

THE TREE.

Darkly shook the boughs above us,
  Not a star shone in the sky,
Clouds sailed past as angry shadows,
  Sadly swept the night wind by.
Though the golden prime of summer,
  Chilly was the hour and drear ;
And a sorrow fell upon us,
  For our parting drew so near.

We had come there walking slowly,
  Minutes quick as moments flying ;
All our love—a friendship holy—
  Told we o'er and o'er with sighing.
Heart to heart, with arms encircled,
  Long we clung in sad embrace ;
I could see thy soft eye-glances
  Though the darkness veiled thy face.

I could feel thy bosom heaving,
  Feel my own responsive swell ;
Feel forebodings keen and keener
  Of that cruel word,—Farewell !
Hope put on the shroud of sadness,
  And the moments flew too fast ;
And we dreaded, while we lingered,
  Still the saddest and the last.

So we kept a mournful silence,
  Waiting underneath the tree,
Till it seemed some kind mutation,
  Wrought a kinder sympathy.
If the night wind sounded dreary,
  Sweeping by with hollow moan,—
Was there not in Nature's sadness,
  Tender concord with our own ?

Deep emotions fear the sunshine,
    Shun the moon's serener light;
Brightness oft embitters sorrow,
    Comfort comes with dusky night.
And we felt our hopes revival
    In that solemn scope of gloom;
Like as flowers that pale and timid,
    Only in the darkness bloom.

Then at length, and yet how sudden,
    Came our fatal word—the last;
And I watched with straining vision
    While thou into darkness past.
Fainter every footfall sounded,
    Then I heard the trellis creak;
Still I listened: but, Oh, sorrow!
    Ne'er again have heard thee speak.

Now the tree is dry and leafless,
    And my heart hath known despair;
Yet for me a sweet remembrance,
    Haunteth as a presence there.
There can I recall our meeting,
    There, alas! our lingering pain;
But to taste once more the gladness,
    All would I endure again.

THE BATTLE OF BETH-HORON.

WITH craft and daring boast,
   The haughty Amorite
Came forth with fearless host,
   Confiding in his might,
And leaguer kings with shield and sword,
To stay the warriors of the Lord.

With mail-clad spearmen tall,
   And mighty men of war,
And slingers trained to gall,
   And bowmen ranged afar,
And brazen chariots in his train
Encamped he strong on Gibeon's plain.

From Gilgal's camp in haste,
   All night by Joshua led
Across the darksome waste,
   The tribes of Israel sped ;
And ere the dawn began to glow
They rushed like whirlwind on the foe.

As clouds before the blast
   Fled all that proud array ;
The slayer followed fast—
   And in their sore dismay
They cried to Moloch and to Baal;
But on them fell the dreadful hail.

Swift o'er the mountain's brow,
   By sword and storm pursued,
Down to Beth-Horon fled
   The stricken multitude—
With broken ranks, and headlong flight,
Their only hope the coming night.

The day began to wane,
   Still rung the battle cry;
Then with uplifted hand,
   Spake Joshua to the sky:—
"Sun, stand thou still on Gibeon!
Moon, stay thy course o'er Ajalon!"

The voice of man prevailed,
   The rising moon was stayed;
The sun stood still, and long
   His going down delayed;
So ancient chronicles recite—
Till Israel slew the Amorite,

HOPE FOR ALL.

Hewer in the sullen mine,
Far from day's delightful shine,
Though uncouthest toil be thine :
Who with axe, and saw, and plane,
Ships construct to sail the main ;
Building church, or shaping wain,—
        There is hope for ye !

Ye who, in the seasons' track,
Furrows drive on earth's broad back,
Reaping sheaf, or piling stack :—
Who vibrate the weary loom
In a damp and dingy room
By a lamp's unhealthy fume,—
        There is hope for ye !

Ye who busy needles ply
Days and nights despairingly,
Sewing ever wearily :—
Ye who tend the cotton-reels,
Whirling as a thing that feels,
See ye not a soul in wheels ?—
        There is hope for ye !

Ye who guide the steam-urged car
On the iron path afar,
Heading mind's aggressive war :—
Who the roaring furnace tend,
Make the stubborn metal bend,
Mould it to a potent friend,—
        There is hope for ye !

Ye of colder heart than head,
Finding—whatsoe'er be said,
Nothing better worth than bread :—

Mark what independent thought
Oft despised and set at naught,
Toiling through all time hath wrought,
    Hope shall conquer ye!

Bards who teemful Nature's looks,
Forests, hills, and running brooks,
Scan, and set in glorious books;
Who amid the human throng,
Find the themes for thought and song,
That stir men's hearts through ages long,—
    There is hope for ye!

Ye who preach, and ye who pray,
Mindful of a coming day,
Catching oft an upward ray;—
Though much still may seem of doom,
Vexëd groping in the gloom,
Buds of Time are yet to bloom,—
    There is hope for ye!

Ruled or Ruler, free or thrall,
Wise or simple, great or small,
Ye who rise, and ye who fall!—
Hope is thought's bright majesty,
Freedom's noblest entity,
Effort's highest energy,—
    Hope is destiny!

THE HILLS.

The hills!—the everlasting hills!
I stand amid their glorious throng,
And breathe new life, the life that fills
The soul with strength, the heart with song ;
And while I view the wondrous sight,
My spirit burns to reach their height.

Tall sentinels whom hoary Time
Hath set to watch in regions lone,
Your welcome to the morning's prime,
Foreruns the sun with trumpet tone ;
And ye in turn around the globe,
Put on your purple evening robe.

Ye have a voice that sounds aloud—
The rushing avalanche appals ;
The echoes of the thunder-cloud ;
The ceaseless roar of waterfalls—
Your anthems these, and winds that sweep
Through all your forests dark and deep.

The Day looks forth and flings his light
On crag and cliff in tinted floods,
And plays at hide-and-seek with Night
Through all your glens, where silence broods ;
The bard—the painter ye inspire ;
But vain they seek to catch your fire.

Rich are your contrasts :—ye bestow
Green alps, and leagues of sombre fir,
And springs of health that ever flow,
And slopes of wine the blood to stir ;
And ores of price, and golden sand,
And stones that lure the sculptor's hand.

Far on your howling wastes of snow,
Lie secret spots of lustrous green,
Where flowers in vivid tincture blow—
A lavish gift of Summer's sheen;
As gems of matchless beauty set
In Winter's icy coronet.

Down from your snows, from doleful caves,
Leap lively rills, rush eager brooks,
Through wild ravines the torrent raves,
Through depths where man's eye never looks;
Yet these erewhile their fury slake
In gentle stream, or sleeping lake.

Aloft stern Winter reigns supreme,
And stretching thence his sceptre forth,
Rolls down a rugged icy stream,
With rigours of the sullen north;
Benumbing, crushing, till his path
Seems but a monument of wrath.

Gleams ghastly through the darksome pines
The frozen chaos pale of hue;
But sweetly in each cranny shines
As from the sky celestial blue:
So creeps he down, and scowls the while,
Till Summer stays him with her smile.

I wander in the lonely glens,
Eyes earthward bent to watch the flowers,
And mosses bright in oozy dens,
And ferns that fashion dainty bowers;
So frail, so delicate, so rare,
As if by angels fostered there.

I hesitate—all is so still;
Shall mortal foot here dare intrude
Where Nature with her freshest skill
Hath formed a virgin solitude?

Perchance e'en lingers yet to see
Her latest page of blazonry.

I stray beyond the flowery sward,
Where rocks oppose the rugged way,
And overhang all tempest-scarr'd,
And grimly bar the light of day ;
There plunges swift the waterfall,
While from the deep hoarse echoes call.

I labour up the cloudy rifts,
And panting scale the rugged brow ;
Another mood now me uplifts—
Mine eyes are gazing skyward now ;
There snow-peaks rise, and while I climb,
My thought lays hold on the sublime.

Here listening sit, though silence reigns,
Faint sounds come floating strangely by,
As of a whisper that complains,
Blown sadly 'twixt the hills and sky ;
Or may we deem that voices speak
Of storm on some far distant peak ?

Below I looked on loveliness ;
Midway on stony masses piled ;
Emotions here my soul possess
Born of the desolate and wild ;
It seems with pain my breath I draw,
These solitudes me overawe.

Memorials of the ages gone,
Of yorework, and of changes vast,
That show us now in every zone,
Strange relics of th' eternal past,
When Nature crude, and lone, and drear,
Lay brooding in a lower sphere.

The ramparts ye from olden days
Of them who slavish suit deny ;

Who dare to live where freedom sways,
And who for freedom dare to die :
Of liberty ye hold the shrine,
O! guard it as a thing divine.

The stains, the flaws, ye thrust aside ;
The scars that on your ranges meet,
Fall off anon, and lower slide,
Till cast away beneath your feet ;
The while your brow of spotless white
Ye rear aloft to greet the light.

'Tis writ that in the days of eld,
The Prophet, on the Arabian Mount,
The Ancient of all Days beheld,
And heard His awful voice recount,
And down from that mysterious place,
Came with a brightness on his face.

So let me bear away with me
Some virtue from the mountains' height,
To dwell within my breast, and be
A witness for the quick'ning light
That born where earth salutes the skies,
Shall me through all my life advise.

A MARRIAGE-DAY RHYME.

Promise, prayer, and blessing spoken,
Clings the golden circlet's token :
One in heart, and one in hope,
One the double horoscope :
Expectation's wayward time
Lost in love's confiding prime.

Heart with heart, and mind with mind
Interwoven intertwined :—
Mingled as the sevenfold ray
Whence proceeds the light of day :
Like as streams that in the river
Meet to flow as one for ever :
Richer now in golden glances
Where the rippled sunlight dances ;
All that gentle is and strong
Poured in one full tide along.

Words seem idle, feeble things
When the soul hath tuned her strings :
What the tongue may fail to say
Will the lips' mute touch convey,
What the heart but ill concealeth
Either clasping hand revealeth :
Reading each in either eye
Secrets of love's treasury :
In every glance a hidden truth
Fraught with tenderness and ruth ;
Love's blind devotion—mystic sense
In high faith merged and reverence.

Life will show as we may guide
Or a dark or sunny side :

Glad as noise of Summer leaves,
Gay as spell that Fancy weaves;
Sweet as roses blossoming,
Joyous as a bird on wing;
Bright as dewdrops on the spray,
Fresh as breezes blown in May,
When the woods their chant begin,
Echo flitting out and in.

Young the heart may ever be,
Life is full of poetry,
Lending e'en to common things
Touches such as sunset flings.
Aspiration conquers care;
Duty hides a moral rare:
Where no lapse inflicts a sorrow,
Oh! how glad each morn and morrow.

Thought with thought, and will with will
Loving ever—linking still;
Two may bear where one would fail,
Each the other's weakness veil.
Twofold shadow—twofold light,
Watchful counsel—hopeful might,
Finding with a fond pretence
Union in a difference:
Each to either heart a test,
Either to the other best.

SILCHESTER.

(Calleva Romanorum.)

O! TELL me not that heart is cold
   Whose thoughts exulting spring
In blooming fields, or leafy woods,
   Where birds their carols sing.

For Nature's scenes pall not the sense,
   Her pleasures never cloy;
Her invitation always is—
   Be happy, and enjoy!

Here, here in God's own temple wide
   My worship shall be given,
In fuller trust, and warmer glow
   Beneath the smile of Heaven.

I feel the sunshine on my brow,
   The breeze upon my cheek,
And in the rustling of the leaves
   Hear Nature fondly speak.

From every tree, and bush, and flower
   Sweet sounds of gladness come,
Where cuckoo sings, or warbles thrush,
   Or bees all busy hum.

The holy influence of the scene
   Steals o'er me while I sit,
And to the Beautiful I feel
   My heart more closely knit.

RHYMES.

Such peaceful rapture fills my heart,
    My spirit feels as free
As if swift wings to fly withal
    Were vouchsafed unto me.

Here sleeps a relic from of old
    A gray, and wasted wall:
A melancholy monument
    'Mid Nature's carnival.

My thought flies back, the Past once more
    In vigorous life appears;
And musing, I forget the lapse
    Of eighteen-hundred years.

I see wild woods, and wilder men
    The leafy glades between:
Comes horrid war—a city stands
    Where stood the forest green.

Here Cæsar's daring eagles flew,
    Here marched his legions strong,
Who conq'ring came to civilise,
    And dignify the wrong.

Still curve yon hills the distant sky,
    With gentle sink and swell,
As when forth from this rampart gazed
    The Roman sentinel.

The spring still flows; but where are they
    Who planted here a home,
And temples built, and shaped the roads
    Whose farther end was Rome?

The men are gone, their works decay,
    And fall beneath the plough;
The spring that bubbled up for them,
    Still lives and sparkles now.

All, all are gone, yet still remains
    The splendour of their fame ;
A language and a law to bear
    Thro' ages long their name.

What contrast ! from the quaint church-tower
    Slow peals the Sabbath bell,
Where cruel games held sway, and where
    The gladiator fell.

And where the Pagan altars glowed
    With sacrificial blaze,
Now rises up the sacred psalm,
    The God of God's to praise.

Thus give we in the breezy weald
    Free play to roving thought ;
Delightful now, anon subdued,
    With solemn teachings fraught.

No forms conventional for me,
    No dictates of the schools
Whose worship never soars above
    A timeworn scheme of rules.

As though the heart for upward flight
    A mechanism required !
No Teacher had, no striving felt,
    Could be no more inspired !

As though th' Eternal dwelt within
    A consecrated wall !
And only bless'd the few who there
    On easy cushions fall.

As though the goodness that pervades
    Creation, Time, and Space
Restricted unto favoured spots
    His efficacious grace.

On moorland waste, on teeming field,
  His dew alike descends ;
The lowly and the lofty ones
  He equally befriends.

And Labour's sons may therefore say—
  'For us are fields and flowers ;
We feel at least one day in seven
  That Providence is ours.'

Up, home! adown the western sky
  The sun is sinking fast ;
One earnest, parting look, I take
  The longest and the last.

A day of respite have I gained
  Amid life's rude turmoil,
And recollections that will cheer
  Through many an hour of toil.

So tell me not the heart is vain,
  Or undevoutly bold,
That loves to pass a Sabbath-day
  Among the ruins old !

WORK OR REST.

You tell me that you long for rest,
That nothing you can satisfy,
That evermore within your breast
A passion born of energy
Torments you with upbraiding throes,
And mocks your yearning for repose.

You tell me that you long for rest,
That life is short, and effort vain,
That spirit by the flesh opprest,
No lofty purpose can attain ;
That life is but a dreary round
Of pleasure sought, but never found.

The better ever is to come—
Such is your thought, and you gainsay
The present, looking eager on
For promise of a future day ;
Sand all of gold, for you—for none
Shall ever through Time's hour-glass run.

Your Present once your Future was
Have all your wishes come to pass ?
Would you evade eternal laws
And what remains at once amass ?
Say, is it true the unpossest
Is better than our present best ?

Fond heart ! that overlooks the good,
The good that comes with every hour,
That faints because her theories
Grow cold when tried, and lose their power ;

As rains that fall in Summer's glow
If Winter sigheth turn to snow.

Best effort still remains the best
Though far below our grand ideal,
And work is better far than rest ;
Storms call out strength that calms conceal.
Faint not, but strive, and trust, and pray—
My strength proportion to my day.

Two lives we bear—one seeming chance
That groweth old—one always young ;
One worn by time and circumstance,
The other ever newly strung
With chords of love for work and truth :
That love enjoys perpetual youth.

Is life a wild experiment
Wherein we mingle cold and hot,
To all result indifferent,
And take, as gamblers take, our lot ?
Nay ! we can help in every test,
And in this truth I take my rest.

TO ADVERSITY.

WITH cruel eye, and visage stern,
As if for victims thou dost yearn,
Why wilt thou still upon me turn :
        What can I more?
What further lesson must I learn?
        Am I not poor?

Teacher, some say, of human kind,
Thou sparest not the lame or blind;
Thy fellows are the bitter wind
        With frost and snow ;
And Hunger creeping up behind
        To hear it blow.

Wouldst thou my cupboard now explore?
No store thou'lt find but only sore ;
And when my children cry for more,
        What shall I give?
O! who with thee to haunt his door,
        Can dare to live?

On all the sky there hangs a scowl,
The stream flows by with sullen growl,
The winds among the chimneys howl,
        And what have we?
No bread, no fire, no fish, no fowl,
        But misery.

O! who shall tell how hard to draw
The line 'twixt Hunger's creed and Law,
When not a crust is left to gnaw,
        And fire is out!
Of justice then, and legal saw
        Who may not doubt?

What ripe inventions hast thou slain!
What grand conceptions of the brain!
What hopes kept ever on the wane,
   And quenched the spark!
What pleasures made give place to pain,
   And light to dark!

'Tis said thou makest clear the sight;
To manhood bringest stubborn might
That cleans the heart from passion's blight
   To inmost core—
Against the wrong to set the right
   For evermore!

This seems to me a crafty joke;
'Tis sunshine buildeth up the oak,
'Tis warmth excites the flax to smoke,
   And wakes the glow:
For one thou'st built thou ten hast broke
   And laid them low.

At first thy visits made me fear,
Drew from my eyes at times a tear;
But since thou cam'st so often here,
   My courage rises;
I know thy ways, thy creeping drear,
   And swift surprises.

I've more than half a mind to try
Which is the stronger, thou or I:
To all thy pinching I reply
   I'll not give in:
And now, indeed, I thee defy,
   In hope to win.

True, if with thee I try a fall,
Thou mayest me so sorely maul,
That I perchance for help may call,
   And call in vain;
Yet take thou heed, whate'er befall—
   I'll try again!

ASPIRATION.

To live for ever!—glorious thought—
   That mortal man a son of Time
   Shall through the ages dwell sublime,
Deep in their wondrous bosom caught :

To live for ever! live and see
   The promise ripen to its hour ;
   The cycles of eternal power,
And all creation's mystery :

To see them with a sense refin'd,
   To read each sun and circling star,
   To scan the future stretching far
With insight of immortal mind,

Seems destiny too great for us
   Who groan in doubt, and hug the chains
   Sin binds us with, and count them gains,
Nor feel our loss in living thus.

Yet not too great ; for He who made
   Came in between us and decay,
   And stampt his image on the clay,
And breath of life breathed in, and bade

To live with everlasting hope,
   But little lower than angels are ;
   And free to overleap the bar
That narrows all the creature's scope.

For ever! shall I then defile
   The soul that lives, and lose my place ;
   And go with shame upon my face
All down the ages—something vile ?

Shall I my aspiration set
   On things that gather present praise,
   On fame, or wealth, or lofty ways,
And all that lies beyond forget?

Shall I, with that eternal spark
   Within me burning—quenchless fire,
   And knowing what is true desire—
Shall I deny, and say 'tis dark?

With altar fires that burn alway,
   The Eastern worshipper adores:
   My worship be the hope that soars
Perpetual o'er the bounds of Day.

A guiding hope, to purge my sight,
   Mine eyes with clearer vision lift
   To solemn portals, where the gift
Awaits us bathed in floods of light.

We see the meanest thing that lives
   Fulfil its purpose in the plan,
   And so through higher grades; but man
Strays, choosing what his freedom gives.

Choose! in the Best thyself acquit;
   Thy Now is pregnant with a Then;
   Thy spirit watch with jealous ken,
Till for the everlasting fit.

RHYMES.

THE ELVES.

A DAY DREAM.

Shone the hot midsummer sun,
Blew the summer breeze,
Wafting through the roaring streets
Whispers from the trees ;
Filling ears that longed to hear
With the hum of bees.

Sweet to leave the daily task,
The city's weary din,
The restless crowds, the pent abodes
Of misery and sin,
And to glad green woods and hills
A pilgrimage begin.

So I wandered through the land,
Sauntering in dales ;
Resting under ruins hoar,
Musing on their tales—
Ever onward till I trod
The mountain land of Wales.

A vague desire—half wish, half hope,
Which oft the spirit daunts,
Yet endures deep down among
The heart's mysterious wants,
Urged me ever on to seek
Nature's wildest haunts.

In the life around there seemed
An inner life to be :

Unseen beings lived I thought
In river, rock, and tree ;
How I longed to lift the veil,
And search the mystery !

Hour by hour throughout the day
Brings a different boon,
A different sense—a different power,
Apt, as may the moon,
Or stars, or dawn, or darkness sway,
Or the burning noon.

With him, I held, who mused and found
" A soul in every thing :"
Yet this soul evaded me ;
Fate o'er all would fling
A darkness thick and dark as that
That frightened Egypt's king.

Give thy heart to quietness ;
Eager quest abate ;
Hearken unto Patience' voice,
Learn to pray and wait ;
Question not of what belongs
To Nature or to Fate.

Whoso waiteth not is vain ;
For sorrow's chastening balm,
And faith's unshrinking steadfastness,
And meditation's calm
Must renew ere hearts can hear
Earth's spirit-chanted psalm.

So I sat on grassy banks
Where the sunbeams fell ;
Knelt to see the daisies blow,
Peep in foxglove bell,
Search the bright and beaded moss
In a dewy dell :

Lingered in a wild ravine,
Awed at Nature's frown,
Where Beauty strove in vain to touch
The masses black and brown,
Where headlong through a roaring rift
A river tumbled down.

I strode from rock to rock, and sat,
And watched the eddies' play,
The plunging swifts, the foaming swirls
That met in noisy fray ;
And voices, while I listened, seemed
Uprising with the spray.

In the forest's shade, I said,
Will the answer come,
Or where on the heather-slopes
Bees honey-gath'ring hum :
Forest, hill-top, heather-slope,
All, all alike was dumb.

Mountain-land I left ; in vain
My hope to penetrate
The mystery of common things :
Oh ! what a weary weight
He bears, who finds no other law
Than iron-handed Fate.

I rested next where meadows green
Salute the loving eye,
Where ancient woods, from upland heights,
Send leafy shelter nigh,
And where between the reedy banks
A river saunters by.

A scene of calm, where stricken hearts
Forget that they are sad ;
Where quiet beauty soothes the mind,
And makes the gazer glad—

That Fancy peoples at her will
With Faun and Oread.

Here and there, through shine and shade
The lily-sprinkled stream
Windeth to the weedy dam,
Where the roar will seem
As is thy mood—a joy, or wail,
Or memory of a dream.

Fulness there of peace and calm
Grassy paths to roam,
Sit, and watch the rapid fall
Rush away in foam—
Morning, noon, or when eve's pomp
Glowed in the western dome.

And runnels underneath the grass
Ran on with merry rout;
And willow-bordered ditches crept
The meadows round about,
With shady nooks, where leaves conspired
To bar the sunshine out.

And many little pools there were
By crooked boughs o'erhung,
Where fishes played among the weeds,
And flitting insects sung;
Where, when the breeze upshook the leaves,
Bright flakes of light were flung.

The life worth living seemed to me,
Stretched on the grass to lie,
And catch through branches overhead
Blue glimpses of the sky:
Forget awhile the eager thought
The one eternal—Why?

Beside the stream, one afternoon
I lay in idle mood,

The fall a distant murmur seemed,
The mill-clack fell subdued ;
When a gentle voice I heard
Speaking from the flood.

I looked, and saw the current swerve
Past a grassy wedge,
While within an eddy whirled
Round a clump of sedge,
And buttercups hung golden fringe
On the water's edge.

Close beside the whirlpool's brim
Curved a little bay,
Where a silver lily-cup
Leaf-encircled lay—
While I looked, in wonder lost,
That chalice seemed to say :—

"An elf escaped to tell of elves,
Offspring of the sun ;
Born in every ray of light
Since his beams begun
To fashion us, and animate
Wherever waters run.

"Of thousand forms, and viewless, we
Dwell in every stream,
Ever at the limpid source
In countless throng we teem ;
Down from ether's limit sent
On every sunny gleam.

"Air or water—brightness there
Thrills us with delight ;
But we mourn, and drift away
Through the dreary night ;
Darkness yields us powerless
To the river's might.

"Most we love our fluent home,
Travelling from the source,
Where the torrent quits the hills,
And with sober force,
Takes through meadows, flower beprankt,
A slow and winding course.

"Rapids swift, and waterfalls
Work us sudden pain;
In their rushing foam and noise
Loudly we complain:
Under a daring salmon's fin
Some leap back again.

"Onward, ever onward still
With the stream we glide;
Soon or late, with stain and slime,
The river rolling wide,
Whelmeth us, a helpless throng,
With the salt sea-tide.

"Then our mood no longer glad
Takes a solemn strain,
And we haunt the lonely ship
Far upon the main;
Tune the waves to lullabies,
For mariners in pain:

"Soothe with chants of woods and hills,
And streamlets far away,
Of cool, green meadows, where the sun
Shines on the new-mown hay,
Of old and quiet churchyards, where
Their bones may never lay.

"Oft the weary seaman hears,
When waves lie asleep,
Voices from his distant home,
Where friends wait and weep:

And he dreads, for these to him
Are whispers from the deep.

" Ocean's wonders—ebb and flow—
And secret scheme we learn ;
We the work of sun and moon,
And polar throb discern ;
Philosophy hath yet, we know,
Much of truth to earn.

" Raging hurricanes we dread,
Shun the tempest's ire ;
Gleam we oft in breezes glad
Bright as sparks of fire :
Yet impatiently we wait
Upwards to aspire.

" When our long probation past
Whirls the misty air,
Lifting us above the clouds,
While the sunbeams fair
Us away to mountain springs,
Brightly bubbling bear.

" Each recall brings fresh delight,
Down the rill we leap,
Hurry through the rocky clefts,
Over caldrons deep,
Cling to dancing bubbles, and
Through their rainbows peep :

" Hasting to the grassy banks
Of cool and quiet meads,
Seeking out the little bays
Fenced by tangled weeds,
Where the old gray willow roots
Strangely show through reeds.

" There among the minnows small,
In and out we creep,

Or, in sandy crevices,
Softly fall asleep,
While between the twisted roots
Gleams of moonlight peep.

" Who the angle loves oft sees
Silvery lacework shine
In the pools o'er which he longs
To cast his cunning line :
He little wots he sees the tracks
Where elves in dance entwine.

" We slide adown long trailing weeds,
Dart through the bent reed's leak,
Seesaw on a ripple's back,
Tasting many a freak,
And in water-lily cups,
Play at hide-and-seek.

" Days befall us—days of calm—
When we idly float
Past the willows, past the meadows,
Past the lazy boat,
While from all the woods around,
Sounds the cuckoo's note.

" Days befall when running streams
Silent seem as glass,
Nature sits with finger up—
Every blade of grass,
And all the trees seem waiting, but
To see their Maker pass.

" Perfect is our gladness then.
Sharing in the rite ;
Adoration gushing forth
To Beauty, Joy, and Might ;
And we, underneath the wave,
Slake ourselves in light.

"Such our life while skies are blue,
But clouds oft hide the sun;
Rivers lashed by wind and storm,
To ocean quicker run,
And water-lilies dip their cups,
Fretful gloom to shun.

"Swept away by yellow floods
In the time of showers,
There we, timid, cling among
Bells of drownèd flowers,
Waiting, chill, the water's ebb,
And the sunny hours.

"Elves have we of wilful way,
Who a tiny nest
Build beneath a pebbly bank,
Seeking there to rest:
Shrinking from their perfect task
In the river's breast.

"These must suffer—some are doomed
To rivers icy cold;
Some down torrents roaring loud,
Wearily are rolled,
Tasked to carry, in the rush,
Countless grains of gold:

"Some to shallow brooks wherein
Oft the waters fail,
Wasted by the Summer sun,
Or the scorching gale:
Then who earnest listens may
Hear them weep and wail.

"Some to horrid pools, whose brink
Blackest water laves;
Some to share the dismal drip,
Deep in murky caves;

Some to creep among the grass
Grown on murderers' graves."

A pause—the sun was sinking low,
I listened yet awhile ;
Could murmurs of the afternoon
My senses thus beguile ?
Then heard a voice as dying song
Steal through a lofty aisle :—

" Who childlike learns to wait and trust,
Works for the work, shall know
The mystery of Nature's hoards,
That live, or lurk, or grow,—
What rules the planet's swift career,
And why thoughts come and go."

Down sank the sun, the millclack ceased,
And, fuller than before,
The stream rushed swifter, and away
The slumb'ring lily bore :—
I listened yet awhile, but heard
That gentle voice no more.

EIGHTEEN-HUNDRED AND FIFTY-ONE.

Grim War had laid his sword aside, and hushed his cannon's roar,
And on his recollections slept, for thirty years and more:—
And save that strife, and fierce revolt had here and there outburned,
And kings had from their kingdoms fled, while thrones were overturned,—
And save that rulers oft had read their simple lesson wrong,
The voice of Peace in many lands spake cheerfully and strong:—
To speak till come that other war, that last tremendous fight,
When Mind all might shall overcome by one eternal Right.

And out of peace great works had grown, and glorious enterprise,
And Science daring matchless deeds put on a fairer guise:
The steamship and the railway-train, the swift electric wire,
To narrow space, and shorten time, and bring the nations nigher—
Came forth from her unwearied toil, her insight keen and vast;
And secrets of philosophy to household uses past.
Free Thought had paced with steady stride, and reached a clearer view
Of social claim, and native worth, and mutual service due.
And Trade had shook his fetters off in consciousness of strength,
And sent a thrill of busy life through England's breadth and length:

And Knowledge stooping from her height, o'erleaped her
 ancient bound,
And fast the steam-fed printing-press diffused her tidings
 round.

Then rose a quick and fruitful thought within a thought-
 ful mind
What if all industries of earth were in one place combined?
The time was ripe, and still the thought to fuller purpose
 grew,
Its greatness over every mind a sense of wonder threw.
The noblest in the realm approved, and royal favour lent,
And England echoed back her will by voice of parliament.
Send out the challenge, make it known, our shores to all
 are free ;
Let labour come from every land, with ships from every
 sea :
Who rarest handicraft can show, and who the simplest
 things ;
Who homely wares for husbandmen, who costly works for
 kings.

Now all ye cunning architects, devise a mighty plan :
A spacious edifice contrive, with roof of widest span.
Since men began to build, the world hath seen no greater
 scheme,
Too high it were for Fancy's flight, too vast for poet's dream.
We need a temple wide and long as any stately street,
With ways and walks of ample scope where all the world
 may meet.
Invention laboured at the task, and with her brooding wit
Devised a scheme of simple art, yet grand, imposing, fit.

Hyde Park the site : straightway is marked the structure's
 spacious bound :
And troops of labourers prepare the broad expanse of
 ground.

And a noise and stir are heard afar of hammer, saw, and plane,
Of whirring wheel, and rolling car, and slowly clanking crane.
And hour by hour the work goes on, increasing day by day ;
A work that tasks all energies, nor brooks an hour's delay.
And soon the nimble artisans beam after beam uprear,
And soon the building's airy lines in lengthening sweep appear.
And glass in endless panels forms a bright, translucent wall ;
The roof, a sky of glass, upborne on iron columns tall.
Above, the lofty gallery, below, the roomy aisle,
And in one length the nave extends for nearly half a mile.
A crystal arch that midway springs, the vista intersects,
And with its wide expanding curve the east and west connects ;
And north and south its radiate arms seem a gigantic fan ;
And ancient elms it covers in beneath its soaring span.
And hour by hour the work goes on, increasing day by day.
A work that tasks all energies, nor brooks an hour's delay.

No Babel this of rash pretence, the vault of heaven to scale ;
No lists where belted knights may ride clad on in linked mail ;
No council hall where learned scribes may talk of doubtful creeds ;
But Industry's high meeting-place, to show his bravest deeds :
Where art with art, and skill with skill, may truly emulate :
Where men may learn what glory most will make the nations great.

Invited then from every land the artificers came.
The humble toiler at the bench, the artist known to fame.
Each brought a labour-tribute there, each claimed a fitting space,
Till all displayed, the countless works filled up the mighty place.

Six months are gone; the task is done, the building stands
   complete ;
Among the labours there evoked, itself the greatest feat.
Now comes the hour of proof and pride, the long-expected
   day,
Through ages dear to English hearts, the gladsome first of
   May.

The day has come, the sun shines out, and all the land is
   green ;
And see where 'mid acclaiming crowds, comes England's
   honoured Queen !
And see what tens of thousands wait around on every
   side !
Each voice repeats the welcome shout, each heart beats
   high with pride.
On every road, and path, and slope, close-thronged the
   myriads stand :
There might be seen the wealth and worth, the strength of
   English land.
The beauty too ; for women came in graceful concourse
   there—
Fond mothers in ripe womanhood, and maidens young and
   fair.
No bayonets gleam, no serried troops in ordered rank
   extend ;
The Queen among the People comes with trust as friend to
   friend.
Hark ! how the myriad voices ring, the echo shakes the
   sky ;
See how the salutations wake as goes the monarch by !

Her presence hailed, the Primate prays for blessing and for
   weal ;
Anon there sounds with chorus full a glorious organ peal :
Swell high the solemn harmonies, sing all with one accord,
Thine be the praise, the triumph Thine, and Thine the
   glory, Lord !

Then thunder-voiced, the cannon spake, and sent the tidings round :
This day a day of mark and note shall evermore be found !
Well may upon the monarch's brow a thoughtful look be seen ;
Of such a people, such a land, how dread to be the Queen!

Few who beheld will e'er forget the grandeur of that day,
The sunbeams flashing on the glass, the banners fluttering gay.
The Spring all glad with flower and leaf, the gleam on every face,
The concord of the multitude, of many-mingled race.
A gathering of the nations there in order and in law :
Oh, 'twas a sight to swell the heart, to fill the mind with awe !

And first there view the spectacle the titled and the great,
And haughty dames, and portly squires, and all the high estate.
Next from each county in the realm, from lands beyond the sea,
The people come ; unnumbered hosts: wide let the entrance be !

And all who enter in are lost at once in mute amaze,
Wonder on wonder meets their eye whichever side they gaze.
The building vast : who would have thought such majesty and grace,
Such startling combinations lay in colour, light, and space ?
While a mighty sound of moving feet goes upward from the floor,
As of ocean waves, that foaming plunge upon a distant shore.

F

There Lancashire shewed woven cloths, there Paisley came
   with shawls,
There carpets hung, and tapestries fit for palatial walls.
And Glasgow came, and brave Dundee, with produce of
   their wheels,
And all the ports of Britain sent the freightage of their
   keels.
There Birmingham and Sheffield came with steel, and
   bronze, and brass,
And Shropshire sent her ironwork, and Sunderland her
   glass.
From darksome depths of earth dug out lay ores for show
   and use,
Hard masses from the crucible, or fibrous veins diffuse.
Northumberland brought lead and coal, and granite Aber-
   deen ;
Came London with a thousand trades, and store of silken
   sheen.
And Staffordshire came there to shew her masterworks of
   clay,
Her pottery's simple excellence, her porcelain's rich dis-
   play.
Here needlework attracts the eye, there painting shews its
   charms ;
Here spreads the bounty of the fields, the produce of the
   farms.
Here gilding bright, and broideries for pageantry and pride,
With implements of husbandry are rangèd side by side.
There ponderous engines stand prepared for haven, mill, or
   ship ;
There locomotives slumb'ring wait, as Titans on the slip.
There oaken carvings seem alive—the hunt, the dog, the
   bird,
And climbing hops, and clust'ring flow'rs, as though the
   wind them stirr'd :
So featly schemed, so kindly touched, it easy were to tell,
The hand and heart that worked thereon, had loved their
   labour well.

There mediæval art revives, there blazoned windows through
The sunlight falls upon the floor, in glooms of wondrous hue.
There telescopes of piercing ken the farthest skies to probe ;
There model ships of swiftest speed, to sail around the globe.

And there apart was shewn the power that England's wealth hath made,
Watt's ever-toiling mechanisms, her underprops of trade.
There Labour with his mightiest arm maintains the ceaseless strife,
With whirl, and roar, and whiz, and hum, and noisy vigour rife.
There to and fro the spinning-frames shew Arkwright's thought matured,
There shuttles fly, there rock the looms, to strenuous task inured,
And ells on ells of warp and web transform from cotton bales,
Weave gauzes light as gossamer, and canvas thick for sails.
There spindles whirling as if mad, spin endless lengths of threads,
There iron shavings from the lathes fall fast as paper shreds ;
There furious saws dance up and down, and pumps out-drain a mine,
There planes sing shrilly as they smooth the solid planks of pine.
Sheet after sheet the printing-press devours with rapid speed,
And sends them forth impatiently, that all who will may read.
Whate'er to old philosophy seemed but a hopeless dream,
Here grows and multiplies beneath the mighty touch of steam.

Whate'er the hand would find to do, whate'er the mind
 desire,
Here manifold machines produce, that linger not nor tire.
With lift, and plunge, and pull, and thrust, so perfectly
 they wrought,
So apt for each emergency, as though the iron thought.

And India with barbaric pomp came from her glowing
 land,
From Himalaya's jungled slopes, to Bengal's torrid strand.
Pagodas there and deities the curious eye engage,
The symbols of a faith come down from earth's primeval
 age.
And all the lavish grandeur that to Rajah life belongs,
Rich chairs and screens of ivory, and palankeens and gongs.
There Canada her bark canoes, her wood, and sledges bore ;
And Borneo sent fragrant gums, and spices Singapore.
Newfoundland and Jamaica came, and all the Western Isles;
Furs from the Icy zone, and fruits from where the Tropic
 smiles.
Ceylon was there, Australia came, New Zealand sent her
 flax ;
And Africa from all her coasts brought drugs, and dyes,
 and wax.

And artisans and weavers came from smoky northern towns,
The miner from his murky pit, the shepherd from the
 downs ;
The quarryman forsook his pick, the fisherman his net,
The delver left the turfy moor—and in the gathering
 met.
Came winsome maidens glad with health, from hamlet and
 from hall,
And bands of hardy labourers, and lusty yeomen tall.
Gray-headed rustic patriarchs came there with tottering
 dames,
And throng of children's children who may keep their
 cherished names.

They came with bag and wallet stored, the tallest and the
  least,
And when their eyes had gazed their fill, they stole aside
  to feast.
It was a happy sight to see their free contented ways,
To see them gather wonder-talk for all their rest of
  days.

In gaberdines and clouted shoon came sunburnt peasants
  there,
In dumb bewilderment they stray, and wildly wondering
  stare.
From cottages on breezy slopes, or snug copse-bordered
  nooks,
Or nestling underneath a hill, which broad domains
  o'erlooks.
From homesteads basking in the sun, 'mid fields of golden
  grain ;
From thatch-roofed homes by village greens, or in the
  straggling lane.
From hidden dales, where brooks in sport leap on the mill-
  wheel's breast ;
From round the little churchyards where old generations
  rest.

They came from Alfred's place of birth, from where he
  fought the Dane,
From where Tintagel's towers look forth across the western
  main.
From where old Caxton lived a boy within the Kentish
  Weald,
From Kenilworth, from Marston Moor, from Worcester's
  crowning field.
From where the Thames upsparkles bright in Lechlade's
  crystal fount,
From where three rivers bubble forth on lone Plinlimmon's
  mount.

From Robin Hood's green forest glades, from famous Runnymede,
From Tintern's hallow'd groves, and where fair Melrose views the Tweed,
From Sidney's stately residence, from Hampden's lowly tomb,
From Chaucer's pleasant haunts, and where dreamt Bunyan in his doom.
Where Cader Idris rears his cliffs, where Snowdon scans the vale,
From where Ben Nevis frowns afar, and braves the northern gale,
From where Dumbarton's rugged walls Columba's Isle discern,
From Killiecrankie's fatal pass, from glorious Bannockburn.
From red Clontarf, the banks of Boyne, Athlone the stout and liege,
And from the hills which long ago saw Londonderry's siege.

And royal blood, and lordly rank, and noble lineage proud,
Relaxed their ancient dignity, and went among the crowd.
They mingled with the multitude that thronged the busy place,
And met with troops of working-men, and looked them in the face.
Henceforth may one eschew distrust, the other cease to scorn,
And learn how much in common binds the high and lowly born.

Look on, ye idle ones and see what Industry can do!
Mark what results from thinking heads and toiling hands accrue.
And see in all the handicraft, in all the works you scan,
The worker hath his merit too, his fame the artisan.
And Labour claims his ancestry, no mean unworthy boast,—
Back-reaching to the earliest days, a great uncounted host.

And France came there in gallant trim, with emulation
 shrewd,
And shewed in all her industry her fitful, pliant mood.
With tapestries of high renown, and porcelain unexcelled,
And marquetry grotesque and grand, on costly tables
 held.
How chastely elegant her forms! her tracery how gay!
Had Fancy in her sportive mood delighted there to
 play?
Her sculptures full of gaysome life, or deep angelic calm:
Be hers the lot in touch and taste to bear away the palm.

There came the patient Hollander, the persevering Dane,
The Belgian with his thrifty skill; and there were brought
 from Spain
Gigantic jars, and jewelled shrines, and rare Toledo blades:
There cloth, and mats, and coronets wove by Tahitian
 maids.
With pipes and muslins Turkey came and decked a gay
 bazaar;
Within the Moslem sate, aloft the Crescent shone afar.
And China came with wondrous toys contrived with crafty
 hand,
And merchandise revealing all her passive Tartar land.
There Tunis pitched a Bedouin tent, and strewed her choice
 perfumes,
Hung Moorish mantles, gaudy fans, and nodding ostrich
 plumes.
There Norway from her peasants' hands sent quaintly
 carved bowls;
With ironwork and porphyry, the Swede his name enrols—
Dug from the rocks where Odin trod in hero-days of yore,
Where Thor his mighty mallet hurled, and made the
 welkin roar.
Greece honey from Hymettus sent, and cloaks and belts
 enwreathed,
And marble blocks like those that once, when Phidias
 touched them, breathed.

And from the frozen north there came the supple
  Muscovite,
With hides, and hemp, and polished ores, and sledges
  gaily dight ;
And rarest gems so bright of hue, that sparkled, gleamed
  and shone
Like tinted flakes from rainbows dropt, and hardened into
  stone ;
From where in drear Siberian wilds the captive mourns
  his ban,
From bleak Archangel's misty shores, from sunny Astra-
  kan.
Vienna shewed her handicraft in proudly furnished rooms,
And Saxony her webs and yarns, and trophies of her
  looms.
And Switzerland, and Italy, in cunning trades combine,
And matchless art with teeming toil, the German
  Zollverein.

There came the keen republicans from that great Western
  Land,
Which peopled from our English soil, flung off her parent's
  hand ;
And brought such proofs of enterprise, such specimens of
  skill,
As shewed the old blood in their veins flowed warm and
  loyal still.
The New World comes to meet the Old, quick youth with
  age to cope ;
To test the prestige of renown, by energetic hope.
She comes from where the Atlantic sea her eastern border
  keeps,
And where towards the setting sun the broad Pacific sleeps.

And men from every country came and went the host
  among,
And nations met and mingled there who spake with
  different tongue,

Yet saw some kindred sympathy, in each some germ of
   good—
More than we thought within us live the ties of
   brotherhood.

Day after day unchecked, unspent, in-poured that eager
   throng,
All through the spring and summer-tide, till autumn nights
   grew long :
And still increasing day by day, the numbers higher rose,
From tens of thousands at the first, to millions at the
   close.

And solemn thoughts come o'er the mind that lingers to
   explore ;
Scene after scene of history returns to view once more.
Range through ! reflect how much we owe the living to
   the dead,
While faint, and faint, and fainter falls the crowd's
   departing tread.

Bless England, Lord ! guide Thou her ways, let People,
   Prince, and Queen
Remember what our England is, and what she long hath
   been.
A land where Freedom's eye unbent hath met Oppression's
   frown,
Where Freedom's hand hath dared to strike the foul
   oppression down.
Where liberty our birthright is—no empty, vaunting name ;
A thousand years of patient growth may well endear its
   claim.
Where champions for the right have come alike from high
   and low,
De Montfort for the parliament, for right of speech De Foe.
A land of language ripe and rich alike for heart and tongue,
Where Wycliffe preached, where Shakspeare wrote, where
   Milton mused and sung.

A land of generous sympathies, whose children love to see
Their fellow-men, in other lands, free as themselves are free.
The mother she of colonies where England's name and worth,
Shall with her Anglo-Saxon tongue be heard throughout the earth ;
From either Pole, through every zone, conjoining at the Line,—
An Empire whereupon the sun looks with perpetual shine.

Our Birth-land this! around her shores roll ocean's sounding waves ;
Within her breast our fathers sleep in old heroic graves :
Our Heritage! with all her fame, her honour, heart, and pow'rs—
God's gift to us, we love her well, she shall be ever ours!

EREBUS AND TERROR.

" Who can stand before His cold?"

I.

Two ships sailed forth, up to the north,
    Up to the north sailed they ;
When fields were green, and hedges white,
    In the pleasant month of May :
Across the sea, till they met the ice
    In the heights of Baffin's Bay.

Through pack and floe still sailed they on,
    Through drift's long rolling chain,
'Mid wondrous shapes of toppling bergs,
    Through many a surging lane ;
Their last of friendly faces saw
    Where dwells the hardy Dane.

And on, still on : blue rolled the sea ;
    No night upon them fell,
Unsetting shone the summer sun,
    And the seamen laughed, for well
Would they the icy rampart force ;
    Where others failed—excel.

They bode no grief, proud in their chief,
    A right good leader he ;
Of gentle word, and steadfast deed,
    Inured to jeopardy :
Who once from Death, o'er arctic wilds,
    Escaped with two or three.

So north and westward sailed they on,
    At midnight still 'twas day ;
Of all the famous Englishmen
    Who thereto made essay,
For full three hundred years and more,
    None more renowned than they.

The farthest whaler's daring sail
    Upon that lonesome sea
They left behind : the whalemen cheer'd
    Good speed! full lustily :
Far-floating seem'd that lusty cheer,
    A dying wail to be.

Still farther on, still farther on,
    The starry Wain beneath ;
Where ice a thousand winters old
    Resists the summer's breath ;
Where cliffs repel e'en moss and snow,
    And seem the throne of Death.

Where summer from the surly ground
    No gladsome Hail! receives ;
Bird never warbles, never sounds
    The noise of rustling leaves ;
Where Nature, doom'd to sullen moods,
    In desolation grieves.

The short-lifed summer drew to end,
    The long bright day was o'er,
And screaming flew the ptarmigan,
    To seek a southern shore ;
And o'er the land, and o'er the sea,
    A chill crept more and more.

The long, long, longer night rushed on,
    And winter grim and drear,
When noon is dark ; and weird-like shapes
    In the white frost-smoke appear ;

And a deep, deep silence reigns, and Death
  Seems creeping very near.

And spectral gleams, and streaming lights,
  Dance in the polar sky :
Strange whispers through the silence come,
  At times a hollow cry—
As if the strong sea spurned his chains,
  And groaned in agony.

The distant hills look ghastly pale,
  As giants in their shroud ;
Stars twinkle in a sky of steel :
  And all with life endow'd
Appalled, shrink close within their ships ;—
  Some fear to speak aloud.

II.

Three winters past, and eager eyes
  Watched at the western strait—
" Come forth ye gallant mariners !
  Here amplest welcomes wait."
No ship came forth, no voice replied,
  Fond hearts fell desolate—

" Oh ! where the chief ? " they cried ; " too long
  Doth England dread his loss ;
Where he who sailed the stormy zone
  Beyond the albatross,
And spied the ice-ribbed mounts of fire,
  Beneath the Southern Cross ? "

Then England sent her succours forth,
  Ships—searchers, many a band,
From east and west as quick to search,
  As 'twere a southern strand ;

And one—one of that two or three,
　　Went searching overland.

From Hendrik Hudson's river sail'd,
　　Strong help our kindred bore ;
France sent a hero-seaman there,
　　Whom France shall see no more ;
And Russia bade her fur-clad tribes
　　Watch on her northern shore.

Among the searchers went the best
　　That England's sea had bred ;
Year after year the search went on,
　　While deeper grew the dread :
At last, an anchorage and graves
　　Revealed that some were dead.

And that was all : in English homes
　　Was heard the long-pent wail,
Where wives and sisters weep bereft ;
　　The maiden turning pale,
Now knew why she had seemed to hear
　　Groans in the northern gale.

Year after year, while Europe heard
　　Swift Revolution's tread,
And saw a palace built to Peace,
　　Anon, War's beacon red :
Still, still the Ice-King mocked, and all
　　We knew was—some were dead.

O wife, that art a widow now,
　　Now let thy sorrow speak !
Let fall, O maiden, waiting long,
　　Thy tears, nor deem them weak !
Good mother, thy first-born no more
　　Shall kiss thine aged cheek.

Oh, then resolved a loyal wife—
   The chief's true wife is she—
A little ship she sent, once more
   To search that lonesome sea :
To save the lost, or relics seek,
   And clear the mystery.

Since first the two lost ships sailed forth
   Had fifteen summers fled,
When came that little ship to port,
   And fearful tidings sped :
Alas! for chief and mariners,
   For all of them were dead.

III.

Oh, hapless, hapless tale to tell !
   A tale to bend the knee :
No sadder fate e'er yet befell
   In any land or sea :
A tale to melt the heart in tears —
   Of utter misery.

How they had left the anchorage,
   To them a peaceful fold ;
And battled with the horrid ice
   A thousand winters old ;
And bore themselves like men, and dar'd
   The cruel, cruel cold.

How, fast beset in high-piled ice,
   Their second winter past,
Where ridgy masses heaving up
   O'ertop the lofty mast ;
And the Ice-King laugh'd, ha! ha! and said,
   " Now are they mine at last."

How in that long, long night of fear
　　The gladness fled their eye;
How proud men stricken by disease
　　Would hide themselves to sigh;
And wounds long-healed once more did gape;
　　And more of them did die.

How when their third of summers came,
　　Ere yet the ships were free,
Death took their chief away, and left
　　Them in their jeopardy:
They buried him through riven ice,
　　Deep in that lonesome sea.

Oh, how they struggled to escape
　　The slowly-drifting ice!
No fitful hour of summer warmth
　　Could them from toil entice:
But the Ice-King laugh'd, ha! ha! and held
　　The ships as in a vice.

Again the long, long winter came,
　　And nipt them far from shore;
And now they droop'd, for summer ne'er
　　Had cheated them before:
'Twould have been music in their ears
　　To hear the billows roar.

In April when the cuckoo chants
　　The gladsome news of spring
In every English woodland glade,
　　They quit their ships, and bring
Five score and five to shore:—o'er some
　　The Angel flapped his wing.

Across the horrid ice they toil'd,
　　Slow toiled they to the land;
There in a cairn the record left,
　　That tells th' escape they plann'd:

The record which the little ship
  With relics, brought to hand.

Then forth along that barren coast,
  While wintry breezes blow ;
Now boat and now sick-laden sledge
  Slow dragging, on they go.
Alas, for sick men who at night
  Rest in those wastes of snow !

Their weakness chilled them with dismay ;
  Can they but reach the main—
There fondly think they succour waits
  To cheer their hapless train :
Once there, Hope whispers they may see
  Their native land again.

Weak still, and weaker day by day,
  They staggered here and there :
In heaps they huddled, hoping warmth,
  But Death lurked in the lair ;
Can men with souls survive on coasts
  Forsaken by the bear ?

That pleasant May ! how long to them
  Seemed since their sail began ;
Now, shivering in the summer sun,
  So wretched and so wan ;
You would have said, had you them seen,
  Can these be brother man ?

With shrunken limbs, and tattered garb,
  With haggard look and worn,
They wandered o'er the dreary waste—
  The dreary waste forlorn ;
And some of them did rue the day
  That ever they were born.

G

And some knelt down and tried to pray,
   But Hunger choked their prayer ;
Some sobbed and wept half-frozen tears
   That brought no sooth to care ;
And some, they on the others look'd
   With eyes of wolfish glare.

Fierce Hunger stared them in the face,
   Grim Famine mocked their schemes ;
Oh, how they thought of their dear home,
   Which aye with plenty teems !
And Hope, life's last and sweetest friend,
   Came to them but in dreams.

Some cursed the earth for barrenness ;
   A wild, reproachful eye
Some raised aloft—'O God, our God !'
   In agony they cry—
'Wilt Thou the manna and the quails
   For evermore deny ?'

Despair woke with them in the morn,
   With them walked side by side
All through the weary day, with them
   Lay down at eventide ;
And some that lay them down to sleep,
   They laid them down and died.

Quit boat—quit sledge—quit all that lags
   Upon their southward way ;
Fall'n towards the south, their skeletons
   In after years still lay ;
As searchers from the little ship
   Beheld with sore dismay.

O, blessed, blessed south ! the land
   Of ever glowing sun !
Where forests teem, and corn and wine,
   Where rivers ever run ;

Where life seems over-full of life
   Still spinning, never spun.

And southward still that lessening band
   Their weary journey trod ;
And one by one they fell and died
   Upon the starvèd sod ;
And the last man sat him down to wait,
   And gasped a prayer to God.

Weep not as hopeless, for their names
   Shall live on Fame's fair scroll :
Her seed of men hath England sown
   In all the seas that roll,
In lands of every zone, and now
   The nearest to the Pole.

WILLIAM TELL.

A POEM FOR CHILDREN.

CANTO I.

It chanced upon a summer day
I sat beneath a leafy tree;
Around ran girls and boys at play,
Hither and thither joyously.
Their shouts of gladness rose and fell,
And pleasant task it were to tell
   Of all their sport and glee:
But speeding from the active throng,
A happy boy came swift along,
   And halting at my knee—
He laid his hand upon my book,
And said, with childhood's wistful look,
"You promised us another tale,
Oh, tell it now; you cannot fail;—
A story for a summer day,
Will be delightful, after play."

"Go call the rest," I said, and soon
   Each happy lad and lass
Was seated, all expectant, on
   The daisy-sprinkled grass.

Dear children, yes—I know a tale,
Will make your little cheeks grow pale;
And from your eyes the tears shall flow,
To hear of suffering and woe;
And then your hearts shall proudly burn
Of noble deeds and thoughts to learn:

How men maintained their native right,
Against a haughty tyrant's might :
How humble hearts may yet be free,
And dare and do for liberty.

'Tis near six hundred years ago
  The Austrian Emperor Rudolf died ;
And left his pride, and pomp, and show,
  And all his empire far and wide
To Albert—one of princely fame,
Yet rests a blot upon his name :
Rudolf had gained the people's love,
But Albert cared no faith to prove ;
His passion knew nor bound nor bar,
He loved not gentle peace, but war.
Had he been wise he would have known,
The truly great leave war alone,
And he perchance had 'scaped the strife
When envious kinsmen took his life.
For lust of power oft sorrow brings,
And teaches while it humbles kings.

Now at that time in Switzerland,
Where snow-capt mountains proudly stand,
There dwelt a loyal-hearted race,
Who tilled the fields, and led the chace.
Their manners simple, wants but few,
Their nature brave, their courage true.
Far down in deeply-sheltered vales,
Or on the slopes of rocky dales,
Or high upon the mountains rude
Brown rustic cots—their shelter stood.
And sweet affections round each hearth,
And freedom's virtues there had birth ;
True guardians of their native home,
Whatever foes or dangers come.

But Uri, Schwyz, and Unterwald—
These three the Forest Cantons called,

Did most for liberty aspire,
And glow with patriotic fire:
Each was to each a trusty friend,
In weal to serve, in woe defend.
No servile art was theirs to bring
False homage to a potent king:
For justice, mercy, truth—alone
Can knit a people to a throne.

With envy Kaiser Albert saw
These people's land, and sturdy law;
He longed to make their hills and plains
A portion of his own domains.
He tempted them with crafty speech;
But they of ancient treaties teach:
He sought to purchase them with gold,
They spurned his proffers brave and bold.
In anger, then, he sent a threat;
But nobly they his envoy met,
And showed the archives of their land,
And vowed the intruder to withstand.

More fiercely kindled Albert's wrath,
To meet such firmness in his path;
Nor did he shrink from further wrong,
For they were weak and he was strong.
So sent he rulers in his name,
The Cantons' hardy pride to tame:
And Gessler came, and Beringar,
The joys of peace to mock and mar.

To Uri Gessler came as lord,
 To spread his master Albert's sway;
Nor spared he either fire or sword,
 To force the people to obey.
Such sternness in his heart he brought,
'Twere sad to tell the woes he wrought:
He tortured men, and wives, and girls;
He called them base-born peasant churls.

"I vow," he said, "their roofs shall smoke,
And on their necks I'll fix the yoke.
Shall they who tend but goats or kine
Against my searching law combine?
Their vaunted pride shall end in shame;
The dungeon shall their spirit tame."

The Unterwalders murmured then,
Through Schwyz a voice in every glen
And Uri cried, with all her men,—
  "How long shall we be slaves?
Better than bend a servile knee,
Forget what freedom's pleasures be,
Or honest thought suppress, that we
  Were sleeping in our graves!
Shall bondage fetter us who scale
The heights where eagles breast the gale
  With proudly-beating wing?
Nay! we appeal to One on high,
In whose sight men all equal lie—
  The peasant and the king:
Till hill and dale, and rock and plain,
Our land shall be our own again."

In lonesome places, hid from sight,
They met, and counsel held at night.
Yet in their half-despairing need
No thought had they of bloody deed;
For virtue waits and suffers long,
Before it renders strife for wrong.
The Emperor they besought that he
Would leave the Forest Cantons free,
And Gessler, whom they feared, recall,
And no more bring them under thrall.

Upon the Unterwalden hills
  Stood Melchtal's free and happy dwelling;
His name was one that love instils;
  Each tongue was of his virtues telling.

All listened to his counsels sage,
The ripened judgment of his age:
Well could he soothe, restrain, advise;
For long experience made him wise.
Wrong seemed less wrongful when he spoke,
And passion less impetuous broke.
He helped the weak their woes to bear,
His bounty did the needy share;
His equals found his friendship true;
And well the tired wayfarer knew
A welcome's ever ready proof
Beneath the honoured Melchtal's roof.

He had a son—an ardent youth,
Of dauntless heart, and lip of truth.
And he was held in high report,
For manly toil, and manly sport:
Alike to labour or to lead,
In pastime or in gallant deed.

In Unterwald Beringar's power
Caused many timorous hearts to cower:
He sent his guards with willing zeal
To pillage through the land, and steal;
And what they would they bore away,
And bold was he who dared gainsay.
One day young Melchtal in the field
Heard the command, "Thy oxen yield!"
And turning round in hasty mood,
Saw where Beringar's archer stood.
With ready speech and honest pride,
And flashing eye, the youth replied:
"What words are thine? and who art thou,
Wilt loose the oxen from my plough?"
The guard a scornful answer made,
And then to loose the beasts essayed.
"Is't come to this—that we must give
Our goods, to help marauders live?"

Young Melchtal cried; and seized the goad,
And such a stout resistance showed;
The archer trembled for his life,
And fled to shun the sudden strife.
The youth sped homewards to relate
How he had turned the threatened fate;
Rejoicing that he dared withstand
The power of strong aggression's hand.
"What hast thou done?" his father said.
"Think'st thou the vengeance to evade?
No hope for thee but instant flight,
Far from the fierce Beringar's might.
To Uri haste,—our friends will bear
Thee safely in concealment there."

Woe was the parting—son and sire—
The victims of oppression dire:
And as they spake the sad farewell
It sounded like a boding knell.
The youth had scarce departed when
The house was thronged by armëd men;
They with rude hand and brutal word
Bore off old Melchtal to their Lord:
Regardless of his many years,
And mocking at his servant's tears.
Then cried Beringar, "Where's thy son?
Speak, traitor, if my wrath thou'dst shun!
My messenger he dared resist,
As though the law were as he list.
Is he the master here, or I?
Know'st thou old man, the penalty?"

Calm in reply old Melchtal said,
"I know, dread Lord: my son hath fled."
"Fled!" cried Beringar, in a rage,
"Old man, say whither? or thy age
On which thou fondly may'st presume,
Shall not protect thee from the doom."

Melchtal replied with fearless tongue,
"Old, weak am I; my son is young:
His life is better worth than mine,
For him I glad myself resign.
The secret shall my heart conceal,
A treasure for our country's weal."

He paused and fixed his bright blue eye
On the chief's face with dignity.
The tyrant answered—" Be it so:
Where hides thy son we yet shall know.
But all thou hast is confiscate,
The law awards it to the state.
Judge if your boasted liberty
Will aught avail in beggary.
Ho! guards, there, bring the pointed steel;
These traitors must be made to feel."
The guards obeyed—Oh! dread surprise:
They pierced the aged Melchtal's eyes;
And closed them up in endless night,
No more to see the blessed light.
Now must he, blind and homeless, stray;
Grope through the land his trembling way.

The cruel deed was done; but vain
Such deeds true virtue to restrain:
Though Melchtal now was blind and poor
Yet found he friends and refuge sure;
And he was loved and solaced still,
And honoured for his lofty will.
And through the land this cruel wrong
Resistance roused more stern and strong.
Thus men who with fierce passion aim,
Oft find their purpose end in shame.

But further must I now relate
Of Gessler's power in Uri state.
He to the town of Altorf went,
Revolving on some dark intent;

Some new invention in his thought,
With danger to the people fraught.
Well might their spirit sink and fail ;
For there he built a gloomy jail ;
With stony dungeons, cold and drear,
For such as talked of freedom near.
None dared to sing their native songs—
Recall the past—recount their wrongs—
But they must lie in dungeon deep,
And there in hopeless sorrow weep :
Their only crime that they should dare
To think, and then their thought declare.

Of somewhat, now, I come to speak—
A ruler's strange, ignoble freak :
For Gessler in the open space
Of Altorf's ancient market-place,
His archers bade a pole erect—
Whereby to test the folk's respect.
And on the top—with craft, mayhap,
He hung the Austrian ducal cap :
A sign, as one might truly deem,
That Austria's power there reigned supreme.
And then proclaimed by beat of drum,
That all who near the pole should come—
Should bow, and humble reverence bear,
As though duke Albert's self stood there :
While near at hand the prison lay,
For such as dared to disobey.

The people heard ; but murmured more,
Firmer of purpose than before.
By reckless insult caution taught,
Among them went the whispered thought ;
For guards were set, the mien to trace
Of all who crossed the market-place,
With order every one to arrest
Who heeded not the lord's behest.—
But here, awhile, must intervene
A homely and a happier scene.

CANTO II.

The dawn is redly beaming
　Far in the eastern sky;
The rosy rays are gleaming
　Across the snow-peaks high:
And streaks of light are twinkling
　Adown the waterfall—
Hark! how the bells are tinkling,
　As loud the herdsmen call.
Up to their mountain meadows,
　The early kine are going,
The vale yet sleeps in shadows,
　While light above is glowing.
The hunter seeks the hill-top,
　The peasant drives his plough;
For brightly into Burglen
　The sun is shining now.

We, children, such a song might sing,
Could we behold an Alpine spring;
When winter yields to sun and showers,
And buds, and leaves, and blooming flowers.
But I my tale must now pursue—
And first another scene we view
Of homely joys and rural life,
Far from the town and all its strife.

Southward from Altorf lies Burglen,
　Deep hid the hills among,
Shut in by soaring mountain heights,
　By lofty crags o'erhung.
And here and there, on slopes of green,
The quaint old houses may be seen;
Or perched upon some grassy knoll,
Or turfy shelf, on cliff's high wall;

And some with signs of rural ease
Stand snugly sheltered by the trees.
That early blooming, hail the spring,
And still their autumn fruitage bring.
And leafy woods on every side
The mountain's lower prospect hide ;
And gladden with their tinted screen,
What else would be a barren scene.
Near by, with rapid stream and strong,
A mountain river foams along,
As though in haste its course to take,
And mingle with the distant lake.
Its noisy splash in summer's heat
With coolness seems the dale to greet :
In winter storms its hurrying roar
Sounds hoarsely on the rocky shore :
The peasant hears the dismal sound,
And tells of hapless travellers drowned.

Burglen in olden time more rude,
More hidden in its solitude,
Was home and shelter to a few
Of Uri's hardy peasants true.
Rude health was theirs, which toil confers
On simple-hearted villagers.
And theirs the joys that every day
The needful duties well repay.
Some at the break of early morn
Blew lusty music on the horn,
When at the signal came the kine,
With tinkling bells along their line :
Them did the wary herdsmen guide
To pasture on the mountain side.
And others drove the timid flocks
To crop the grass among the rocks ;
While hunters all the ground explore
For prowling wolf and hungry boar ;

Or watchful sudden arrows speed
At eagle fierce or screaming glead.
Each man could use his trusty bow,
And each a varied art could show;
To shoot, or fish, or till the soil—
Skilled either for defence or toil.

And nooks there were that children knew,
Where flowers in wild-blown sweetness grew;
And there beneath the forest-shade,
Blithe groups of village children played,
Or pensive youths and maidens strayed,
   In life's sweet wayward pride.
At times it seemed the sultry breeze
Would linger 'mid the branching trees,
And list while flower-roving bees
   Hummed in the summer tide;
Then forth would sweep, uncaring where,
And flood with freshness all the air.

And near at hand the chapel stood,
Whose bell inspired a reverent mood,
Brought old and young, with heart subdued,
   Attendant on its chime:
There some had paid the marriage vow,
With flowers enwreathed upon their brow,
And loved as well and truly now,
   As in their gladsome prime.
And many on that sacred site
Had borne the blest baptismal rite;
And oft within the ancient walls
Had joined in holy festivals.
And there around the building lay
The graves of others—passed away;
Some even lost to rumour's tongue;
Some still lamented—old and young;
A spot to heal or chasten thought,
With tears of loving sorrow fraught.

When winter came in bleak attire,
On each hearth blazed the winter fire,
High heapèd with the ready store,
That woodmen from the forest bore.
And when the hardy hunters came
At night returned with welcome game
Perchance a deer, or birds of note,
Perchance a noble chamois goat,
Glad cheer it was to see the glow,
While all without was drift and snow ;
And well it was that cheerful smiles
Repaid the rigour of their toils.
Then children crowded round to hear
How flew the dogs, how fared the deer :
How some on treach'rous ice had failed ;
How bravely some the wolf assailed ;
How some had sorely wounded been,
Just as the glancing arrow keen,
Them from his hungry jaws releast,
And slew the gaunt and furious beast.
Much marvelled they it should be so,
And feared to touch their father's bow,
Yet pleased their mimic weapons bring
And fly the arrows from the string.
The parents note their children's play,
And think upon the future day.
And other while some ballad rhyme,
Or legend of the olden time,
Or stories of the saints would be
The night's enlivening history.
At times perchance some minstrel's lay
Of lordly knight or lady gay ;
Or else some pious pilgrim's prayer
Who halted on his wandering there.

Dwelt with these peasants one whose name,
Must now awhile our notice claim
One long to be observed by fame,
   Or thought of as a spell :

He lived in Burglen as the rest,
And neighbours frankly him confest
Among the brave the first and best:
   His name was WILLIAM TELL.
Beneath the roof where he was born
Still saw he rise the golden morn,
Still heard the pealing Alpine horn,
   And lived devoid of care.
And there his household treasures meet,
A wife to make his labour sweet,
Two boys his daily love to greet—
   All these his pleasures share.
Two mountain boys of active frames,
The foremost in the village games.

One day TELL laboured in the ground
That formed his dwelling's frontward bound,
And sturdily his axe he plied
Upon a tree-stem's knotty side.
Yet paused he oft in thoughtful mood,
As though with anxious doubts imbued.
The merry boys were playing by,
Watched by their mother's loving eye;
She notes at length TELL'S frequent pause,
And instant seeks to learn the cause:
" Dear husband! thou wast ever glad;
Whence comes it now thou art so sad?
O! tell me if some secret harm
Hath worked thee to a strange alarm?
What thou endurest I can bear;
Whate'er thy grief, oh, let me share."

" Dear wife! forbear thy boding fears,
Though cause enough there be for tears.
Come sit and listen while I say
Of what befel but yesterday.
Last night with toil o'erspent I came
Thou know'st, and didst my tarrying blame.

"I went to see the ferryman,
   Who lives upon the shore;
And of our country's wrongs we talked,
   And troubles yet in store, —
For oft Kuoni rumour hears,
As folk across the lake he steers.
And there he told me of a deed,
   That made my flesh to creep:
And he, the rugged ferryman,
   He could not choose but weep.
Old Melchtal—he of Unterwald—
   Thou bearest him in mind—'
Is now a hapless fugitive,
   Want-stricken, feeble, blind.
The tyrant's minions pierced his eyes,
   And but for friendly aid,
Melchtal the loved, the good, the wise,
   Must ply the beggar's trade.
Well may'st thou shrink at such a sin,
   And done by human hand:
God pardon them—for few there be
   Will pardon in our land!
Sorrow and anger ruled by turns,
   As old Kuoni spoke;
And while we mourned, and chafed, and schemed,
   A sudden tempest broke.
Fierce blew the blast, upheaved the lake,
   And 'mid the waters' toss,
Cried from the farther shore a voice—
   'Haste, ferryman! across.'
Kuoni feared the angry storm;
   Down to the boat I ran,
And thanked be Heaven who aided me,
   I saved the eager man.
It was young Melchtal, forced to flee;
   I led with hasty strides;
And now within our Uri bounds,
   He with thy father bides.

I could not tell him of the wrong
    Upon his parent done ;
But left him there, and wandered on
    Impatiently, alone.
Like fire the blood coursed through my veins ;
    And when old Melchtal's plight
Came o'er my mind—unconsciously,
    I clenched my hand to smite.
I wandered on, nor whither saw,
    Such heat was in my brain ;
Far up the rugged Rigisberg—
    The day began to wane :
A driving blast came from the height,
    With blinding snow and sleet ;
And there upon the dizzy ridge,
    I chanced a stranger meet.
He, with a hunting-party gay,
    Went early on the chase ;
But he had strayed, and now in vain,
    He sought the path to trace.
Benumbed and shrinking from the gale,
    Had he been there alone,
He would have died before the morn,
    And none his fate have known.
Yet haughtily he spoke, and said,
    'Ho ! peasant, be my guide.'
At such a time, a man, I thought,
    Might well abate his pride.
'Guide me to Altorf,' next he said
    'Thy service I'll repay :'
I knew him then, but nought replied,
    And turned and led the way.
'Twas Gessler, and at times I thought,
    'Twere best to leave him there :
For, like the Lord of Unterwald,
    His presence brings despair.
But yet I led—at length we came
    In view of Altorf gate :

And there he stoutly questioned me
  About my name and state.
'Thy mien is bold,' he said, 'not such
  As peasants ought to show:
What is thy name? now answer me
  Before I let thee go,'
'Am I thy bondman?' I replied—
  'Do I thy bidding wait?
Lord Gessler, hear, my name is TELL:
  A peasant's is my state.
But one of thousands, haughty lord!
  All trusty men and strong;
Who dare their ancient right uphold,
  And dare resist the wrong.'
He started when I spoke his name,
  And said, as then he turned,
'Come! follow me, and thou shalt have
  The pay thou well hast earned,'
Then answered I, 'my task is done,
  I wait for no reward;
At need bethink thee how one while,
  A peasant served a Lord.'
Whereat he chafed, and suddenly
  Did to the archers call,
Who watched while pacing up and down
  Upon the distant wall:
'Ho! hither guards: this fellow seize:'
  My temper waxèd grim;
My bow was in my hand, and yet—
  I did no harm to him.
I left him standing in the path,
  And homeward took my way:
And now good wife thou knowest why
  My thought is sad to-day."

She listened with attentive ear,
In changeful mood of hope and fear.

At last her tearful eye she raised,
"O, husband dear! now heaven be praised
That thou constrained to nobler good,
The fierce temptation hast withstood.
Thy wanderings for a time defer,
Lest thou some vengeful risk incur;
The Governor's wrath I sorely dread,
For what thou hast so bravely said."

"Fear not, dear wife, I shall be ware
Of lurking foe or crafty snare;
But I must journey forth to-day,
And counsel to our friends convey.
Thy father says our leaguers wait
But for the word to rouse the State.
Wilhelm goes with me, for the lad
E'er makes his honoured grandsire glad.
To Altorf first—to learn if aught
Hath promise to our party brought."

"Nay TELL! go not;" his wife replied,
"Who knows what evil may betide?
In Altorf, too, what risk may be,
Ye both may rue some treachery!"
"No risk, no prize," TELL answering spoke,
"And who, to break a country's yoke,
Would not adventure to the deed,
Doth manly thought and purpose need:
Repel thy fears, thou may'st reflect,
That Heaven can everywhere protect."

TELL reached his cross-bow from the wall,
  A weapon prized and true:
His son tripped lightly by his side,
  And on their way they drew.
With boding heart the mother saw
  Her first-born led away,

And mounting to her chamber, there
  She meekly knelt to pray.
Meantime the two with steady pace,
Came near to Altorf's market-place.
At each approach an archer guard
With lance in hand kept watch and ward;
And TELL, unconscious of offence,
Paid not the bidden reverence.
"Hold!" cried the guard, "how, go ye by;
Nor heed the signal lifted high?
See, where it hangs! the law is now—
That all who pass the cap shall bow."

"Bow to a cap!" said TELL, "who makes
Such laws as even instinct breaks;
And are we fallen so low to be
A mocking jest for tyranny?"

"Ye waste but words in churlish pride:
Salute the cap;" the guard replied.

"Nay," answered TELL, "shall it be told
We sanctioned such an outrage bold?
Think ye, sir archer, that our knees
Are made to bend as tyrants please?
We, nursed in freedom's rugged lap,
Cannot nor will salute the cap."

"Ho! guards, this way, this fellow dares
To question of our chief's affairs;
I trow Lord Gessler will him teach
To hold another sort of speech."
Round TELL and Wilhelm came the throng,
And marched away in circle strong,
And brought them soon—the way was short
Where Gessler held his lordly court;
While angry threats and murmurs loud,
Went through the people's following crowd.

The peasant stood before the lord,
    And bravely met his eye,
As when he on the stormy hill
    Did timely aid supply.
Young Wilhelm saw that glance of fire,
And waited fearless as his sire;
And save the haughty ruler's ire—
    They boded nought of ill.
Their homely garb looked plain beside
The trappings gay of war and pride,
That decked the ranks of those who bide
    The spacious hall to fill:
For some within that vaulted room
Wore velvet robe and nodding plume,
Nor did the glittering armour fail,
The polished shield and coat of mail;
And gilded banners hanging high,
Marked names of proudest chivalry.
Above the rest Lord Gessler sate,
While round the door the archers wait.

When Gessler heard the prompt complaint
Touching his dignity's attaint,
He sudden asked, with frowning brow,
"Ho! base-born peasant, who art thou?"

Tell spoke, while proudly flushed his face—
"The base-born he, whose deeds are base.
Let him be such, who would enslave
A free-born people, true and brave."

"What! wilt thou bandy words with me?"
Retorted Gessler scornfully;
"Evading thus thy lord's appeal:
Thy name and errand now reveal."

"My name thou know'st—when last we met,
Not hastily wilt thou forget.

My name is TELL.—my errand's aim,
Is mine alone: not thine to claim."

"Vaunt not," said Gessler, "but obey:
And to the cap thy reverence pay."

"To free-born men it is not given,
To bow the knee except to Heaven.
Lord Gessler let this question cease,
And order now our quick release."

"And shall I thus the mandate break?
Here more than honour is at stake.
The Emperor's will ye now withstand,
From high to low throughout the land.
If thou would'st freely pass thy way,
At once a subject's service pay."

"Lord Gessler," answered TELL, "can right
Endure the wrongful ways of might?
What thou requirest is a snare,
To make us Austrian bondage bear;
But come what may, I will not bow,
Whate'er the Emperor deem or thou!"

A movement went around the hall,
   At TELL'S undaunted speech;
And here and there one started up,
   Such daring to impeach,
For many of his fame had heard,
   How he with ready hand
Could send his arrow to the mark:
   None truer in the land.

"So, as thou wilt," was Gessler's word,
"Wilt thou the penalty afford?
Hearken, bold peasant, on my breath
Depends thy liberty or death."

"Death? cruel Lord, yes, well I know
Thy heart to mercy's teachings slow :
But death for failing such behest !
In this, forsooth, thou canst but jest."

"This shalt thou judge?" the Lord replied,
"What youth is he stands at thy side?"
TELL heard the words with sudden start ;
The wily question searched his heart.

The father looked down on his boy,
A tear-drop dimmed his eye :
What pretext could he there employ
   To shape the apt reply ?
"Let it content thee, Lord," he said,
   "We love this gentle one ;
And oft he dwells beneath our roof,
   He is –he is my son."

Spake Gessler then, "'tis rumoured, TELL,
Thou every bowman dost excel :
Men say thy aim is sure and stark,
And never fails the distant mark.
Before us thou shalt send a shaft,
And shew a sample of thy craft.
Break up the court, for here the proof,
Admits no strait inclosing roof."

The courtly train then left the hall,
   The troop of archers past ;
And guarded still by watchful eyes,
   TELL with his son went last.
And soon two ranks stood face to face,
Were ranged along the market-place,
As Gessler, from a lofty seat,
Ordered the preparations meet.
TELL felt a proud and gladsome thrill
To know his fate hung on his skill ;

Ere long, he hoped, the trial o'er,
To pass unquestioned as before.

But soon a new command he heard,
That him to deepest anguish stirred :
"Now, TELL," said Gessler, " take thy bow,
And straight to yonder station go.
The boy a bow-shot distant led
Shall stand,—an apple on his head
Shall be thy mark--a noble test ;
Prove well thy aim, and do thy best ;
For if the arrow go astray,
Thy life shall instant forfeit pay."

TELL stood as one transformed to stone,
Or horrid spell around him thrown.
Oh ! was it not some fearful dream,
That dread reality did seem ?
Or was it but a mockery, meant
To prove how steadfast his intent ?

" Gessler," he said, " O ! hear in ruth,
No blame attends this gentle youth ;
He hath in nought offended thee,
And well may prove thy clemency."

The Lord rejoined, " he bears thy name—
'Tis well : thou'lt need a stricter aim."

An archer slowly paced the ground ;
Dismayed the people crowded round ;
A shuddering horror o'er them fell,
To mark the fierce suspense of TELL.
And threats were muttered dark and deep ;
And mothers there were seen to weep.
Young Wilhelm's danger made them sad,
For all who saw him loved the lad,
Who cheered by youthful courage good,
Already in the distance stood.

Who goes to Altorf's market-place,
Full six-score steps may truly pace,
Between two fountains in the space,
   Whose waters leap and play,
And high their bubbling current throw,
And plash and murmur as they flow:
Built to all after-time to show
   Where, on that fateful day—
Two heroes stood—whose like is none:
A hero father—hero son.

The cherished bow to TELL was brought,
He next the offered arrows sought,
And chose a shaft both straight and keen,
And then—he hoped the act unseen—
He stealthily a second drew,
And hid beneath his vest from view.
But few could look upon his face,
As slowly then he took his place;
So painful was the sight to see
That matchless bowman's agony.

Then all his pent emotion broke,
And to his hardy boy he spoke:
"My son, my son, O! woe the hour,
That we became the sport of power!
O! hadst thou with thy mother stayed,
This bitter part thou hadst not played!
O! could she see thee standing there,
What were her anguish—her despair!
How can I aim oppressed with fears,
Foreboding all her grief and tears?"

Wilhelm replied in sweetest tone,
To childhood that belongs alone;
"No danger, father's in thy string,
Thou hitt'st the bird upon the wing;

And far as arrow's flight may be
Wilt strike an apple from the tree.
Oh, fear not, father, for thy skill,
The weapon can direct at will."

TELL raised his cross-bow to the aim,
It seemed his courage went and came;
Yet who will dare the parent blame,
   He still delayed to do?
He looked from eye to eye, and saw,
Here, maledictions on the law;
There, dark resolves that inly gnaw,
   And down his weapon threw:
"Lord Gessler," cried he, "take my life;
Let cease at once this goading strife:
Do with me as thou wilt, but spare
The boy to bless his mother's care."

The Governor in haste replied,
"In vain the plea—thy suit's denied."

Among the crowd there stood a few
Of worthy fame and courage true:
They joined in eloquent request,
TELL might be spared the fearful test.
But Gessler kept his stubborn mood,
Nor could his purpose be withstood.

Said TELL, "I cannot harm my son;
For now he seems my dearest one.
And year by year—from infancy,
His life comes crowding back to me:
The days of all his simple wiles,
The days of all his mother's smiles.—
My heart revolts with very shame
To think of such a murd'rous aim!"

"Dear father, thou hast taught me well
To hold on hope, whate'er befel.

My mother too, when danger near,
Would say Heaven's trust preserves from fear.
Oh, fear not, father, that I shrink,
Thou shalt not see an eyelid wink.
Yon rock, whose summit breasts the sky,
Shall not more firmly stand than I."

" Boy, well hast thou reminded me
Of what befits myself and thee.
If I in thought a moment failed,
If for a space my spirit quailed,
I now can surer guidance ask,
I now can dare the fearful task.
Heaven help us, boy! for such a deed,
Who would not more than courage need?"

The father kissed his son, and then
Paced slowly to his place again;
Yet paused once more at Gessler's seat
To crave remission of the feat:
" Recall," he said, "thy stern decree;
Or work thy will alone on me.
Let children not thy wrath employ:
I'll kneel to thee to save my boy."

With angry taunt the Governor laught,
" Is life less worth than bowman's craft?
Vex me no more: 'tis vain to ask;
Away! betake thee to thy task."

The fire that lights a freeman's soul,
In TELL'S eye flashed as glowing coal,
  And back he strode amain:
He seized his bow, and aiming true,
Loud twanged the string, the arrow flew,
  The apple split in twain;
And as the severed fragments fell,
The people cried—' Hurra! for TELL.'

And who shall paint the father's joy,
To note the safety of his boy?
"O! bravely hast thou stood the test,"
He said, and clasped him to his breast.

But Gessler ill could brook the skill
That thus opposed his deadly will;
The hidden arrow caught his eye,
That TELL had taken covertly:
"How now!" he cried, "more rebels' craft:
Wherefore and whence that other shaft?"
Stept boldly forth, TELL made reply,
"Learn, haughty Lord, if so that I
Had harmed my son—Lord though thou be,
This second shaft was meant for thee."

None stood there by that dared assuage
The Governor's vindictive rage;
"I promised life," he cried to TELL;
"And thou shalt live; but in a cell."
And loud he spoke his stern commands—
"Guards! seize the traitor: bind his hands.
Him with our escort will we take
To Kussnacht's tower beyond the lake."

CANTO III.

The boat was manned as Gessler bade,
Along the lake her course was laid;
But what a mingled freight she bore
From Altorf to the farther shore!
Triumphant power, and malice there,
And servile thought, and weary care,
And doubt of retributive strife,
And fears that dry the springs of life,
Assembled were—a little plan
Of man's accustomed art with man.

Lord Gessler sat, still fierce and grim,
The landscape had no charms for him;
He heeded not the graceful play
Of light and shade, where sunbeams lay.
No charm he saw in clustering trees,
That bowed their branches to the breeze;
Nor heard the lightly sounding splash,
As wavelets on the margin dash.
From time to time his glances fell
Upon his hated victim—TELL,
Who sat with wrist in fetters rude;
His will constrained yet unsubdued.
The iron could not curb his mind,
His thought could rove still unconfined.
Revisiting his household cares,
His wife's, his boys' alarm he shares;
How will they watch and wait for him,
Now sitting there with fettered limb!
He prays heaven shield them yet from harm;
And while he thinks his heart grows warm,
And seems to catch its wonted glow—
But what a fate awaits him now!
He, who could climb the topmost fell,
Now doomed to pine in darksome cell;

He, who could face the wolf or boar,
May scale the mountain peaks no more!
Must light exchange for dismal gloom,
And freedom for a living tomb.

But TELL still hoped in hour of need
To save himself by valiant deed;
Although oppressed by weighty care,
Not his the weakness of despair.
He all around the mountains knew,
That showed their lofty summits blue:
Their changeful outline he could trace,
Familiar as a brother's face.
He knew where foaming torrents fell,
And where reposed the verdant dell;
And while he viewed the rugged slopes,
Came crowding back his youthful hopes.

Yet as he gazed, how changed the view,
A shadow o'er the landscape grew.
The hills put on a misty shroud,
And downward crept the gathering cloud.
Then came a whirl—a hollow breeze,
That, wildly moaning, swept the trees;
Then all was mute—a solemn change—
Yet seemed the stillness drear and strange,
As though some direful presence there
Lay circling on the darkening air;
And waited only for a doom,
To blot the day with tempest's gloom.

Anon there rushed a ragged blast,
That o'er the lake foam-lashing past;
As though a wind, grown tired of play,
In sullen spite had run away.
And thunder, muttering remote,
Seemed like a far-off battle note.
At times a slanting sunny beam
Flung down a fitful ghastly gleam.

And still more fearful seemed the change :
More ominous the portents strange.

But dark the sky and darker grew,
The shrieking blast unceasing blew,
And lightning flash and storm-cloud driven
Sped madly o'er the lurid heaven.
And now the lake's deep waters hurled,
In white and foaming billows curled ;
And like a bird with broken wing,
Or reeling like a drunken thing,
There tossed the boat ; her crew all pale,
Cowered in dismay beneath the gale.
In vain cried Gessler, " Row ! ye knaves :"
They pointed to the surging waves,
That in that wild appalling hour
There mocked his presence and his power.
No help was now in bows or spears ;
And might despaired, rebuked by fears.

And howling still the tempest blew
And high the raging waters flew ;
So giddily the boat was toss'd,
Her crew gave up themselves for lost.
Now rising on a surging swell,
Now into yawning deeps she fell ;
And each man trembled for his life,
So fierce 'twixt wind and wave the strife :
Save TELL, who sat with eye serene,
And spirit calm, and lofty mien :
A good man's thought all fear disarms,
And comforts him amid alarms.

And still the thunderous storm-clouds flew,
And still the howling tempest blew,
At times it seemed with dreadful swoop,
Down on the boiling lake to stoop ;

With fury on the boat to bear—
Anon it swept the upper air.
Then came again that silence deep,
As though the winds had gone to sleep;
Then gust on gust rushed wildly driven,
From every quarter of the heaven,
And hurtling from the mountain shore,
Careered more fiercely than before.

The fury of the foaming lake
Might well the stoutest courage shake.
In vain the crew their labours ply;
The tempest held the mastery;
Now hither and now thither rocked,
As if the storm their terror mocked.
Dark threats in vain, did Gessler urge,
They nought availed against the surge.
Upon the benches sat the crew,
No effort could they more renew:
Their strength was gone, their hope all spent,
Nor whence they came, nor whither went
Could see, for spray and shifting gloom;
And sullen waited for their doom.

While thus they powerless sat in dread,
　And fast their courage fell,
An archer cried, "one hope is left;
　Our only hope is TELL.
Lord Gessler, hearken! he is skilled,
　Beyond all reach of fear:
And well as he can use the bow,
　So wisely can he steer.
O! let him now, from irons freed,
　But take the helm in hand;
I warrant me, Lord Gessler, soon
　He'll bring the boat to land."

The Governor heard, and thought awhile,
    What if the captive should refuse?
Or seek to render guile for guile;
    Or death to loss of freedom choose?
Should he, the ruler in the land,
Seek safety at a peasant's hand?
Or give to liberty again,
The bravest of the mountain men?
Anon his hesitation past;
For unabated blew the blast.
Not mercy made him cling to life,
But further hope of vengeful strife.

So Gessler spake, "If, as I hear,
Thou, TELL, art skilled a boat to steer,
Now at the rudder take thy stand,
And bring us safely to the land.
Thus traitorous speech shalt thou repay,
And pardoned, freely pass thy way."

TELL'S hands were loosed from fetters vile,
He thus acceptance spake the while:
"My life," he said, "is dear to me,
As thine, Lord Gessler, is to thee.
My love a wife and children claim;
And somewhat for my country's fame.
Judge ye, ere-long, as I perform,
What skill may weather out the storm."

On this the hardy mountaineer,
With helm in hand began to steer
And warily made for the shores,
The while the crew resumed their oars.
Within the mountain's sheltering height,
He knew the gale of lesser might.
The boat obeyed the steersman true,
And o'er the surges landward drew;

And guided by TELL's vigorous arm,
The crew forgot their late alarm.
E'en Gessler owned the courage brave,
That triumphed o'er the threatening wave.

But TELL, by shrewd perception taught,
Revolved within a daring thought ;
A purpose lurked within his eye,
Which none there present may descry.
Well might he dread, if he should land
With Gessler and his servile band,
The dungeon still would be his fate,
And he long years a captive wait ;
In dismal night or grisly day,
Despairing linger life away.
TELL's bow and quiver at his feet,
Were placed behind Lord Gessler's seat :
A trophy for the massive wall,
In Kussnacht's gloomy castle hall.

Upon the border of the lake
   Juts forth a rock, low, rugged, bare ;
Where angry waters foaming break
   The traveller still may see it there.
A little chapel marks the place,
   Built in the olden time ;
For well men loved in ancient days
   To hallow the sublime.
Long may the little chapel stand,
   A noble record in the land !

Then TELL, he so adroitly steered,
That to the rock the vessel neared.
With prompt design he dared a deed,
Where only daring can succeed ;
And nearer come he grasped his bow,
His quiver seized—and stooping low,
   Upon the rock he leapt :
And with his foot the vessel spurned ;

Her prow upon the impulse turned,
  And past the rock she swept—
Again to struggle with the blast,
That still blew furiously and fast.

As chafes a tiger in his cage,
So Gessler stormed in baffled rage ;
His passion's heat in curses broke,
Stern maledictions loud he spoke,
On winds that mocked him as they blew,
Upon his archers, boat, and crew.
Vain all the efforts they could make,
The vessel drifted o'er the lake.

TELL, panting with the hasty shock,
Remained yet standing on the rock ;
And in the first brief moments there,
He prayed a thankful spirit's prayer.
By signs he marked the sudden gale,
Its fury spent, began to fail :
Another work remains ere night—
He turned, and climbed the rocky height.

CANTO IV.

The fury of the storm was past,
Less fiercely blew the howling blast ;
The waters tossed less wild and high,
The boat escaped the peril nigh.
The crew at length could ply their oars,
As Gessler pointed to the shores ;
And rowing yet some miles away,
They landed in a distant bay.
Here Gessler no delay could brook,
Himself at once to horse betook ;
His captain too, and archer guide,
Did straight for Kussnacht's castle ride.
On foot the rest their journey take,
Right glad to have escaped the lake.

But TELL, meanwhile, with ready might,
Had gained the summit of the height ;
And paused a space as though he sought,
To strive with some contending thought.
His trusty bow he closely scanned,
To note if ready to his hand ;
He wiped the moisture from the string,
And tried the promptly rising spring:
And thus with satisfaction knew,
His cherished weapon still was true.
He slung his quiver at his back,
And hastened on the mountain track ;
He knew all by-paths many a mile,
Through hidden glen or steep defile ;
Or traversing a turfy slope,
Or o'er some rocky hillock's cope ;
Or underneath the gloomy firs,
Whose top the wind unceasing stirs.
Some secret power seemed him to chase,
So fast and constant was his pace ;

He kept his eye bent on the ground,
And neither paused nor looked around.
What was the purpose thus to need
Such steady persevering speed?

Perchance it was he homeward went,
On sweet domestic joys intent;
But far behind him Burglen lay;
His home was many miles away.
In vain you watched his earnest face,
No passing smile there left a trace;
For glad emotions seemed no room,
Where all looked mingled doubt and gloom.
Whate'er the recollections brought,
They but impelled his sterner thought.

Yet once he paused— and standing still,
Upon the shoulder of a hill,
Beheld within his vision's ken,
The heights that fence his native glen.
In mind he saw the pleasing scene—
His home among the pastures green,
Partook of welcome household joys,
And shared the pastimes of his boys.
He heard their voices, loving strife;
And soothed his long expectant wife.
So far remote, in thought so near;
How peaceful there, how fervid here!
The pause thus to affection lent,
Once more he to his purpose bent;
And paced along his devious way,
While waned the swiftly-passing day.

At length a rocky brow he reached,
O'er which a hollow roadway stretched;
Where rooted broken crags among,
Wild shrubs a tangled shadow flung,

And from each narrow crevice hung
   Thin weeds and scanty grass :
And TELL came on with hasty stride,
Behind the crags he sought to hide,
He knew that Gessler soon must ride
   Along that rugged pass.
Of old it was the public way
That from the lake to Kussnacht lay.

He climbed among the crags and sate
As one resolved that lies in wait.
No wavering purpose had he now,
He gazed towards the rising brow.
While past, on various errand bent,
Wayfarers on the journey went.
One time some mounted trader wise
In traffic's wiles or merchandise :
Anon a daring hunter came
In eager quest of mountain game ;
Or couriers with impatient speed ;
Or beggars tottering in their need.
Herdsmen and husbandmen went past,
And mounted troopers riding fast.
And gaily came a marriage throng
With music and with simple song.
And whiles with toiling penance bent,
A pilgrim paced the steep ascent ;
Seeking perchance some distant shrine,
Some saintly relics deemed divine.
Each had a purpose in his breast—
Pride, love, devotion, trade or jest.

" And mine," said TELL, " is true and brave,
My purpose is the land to save.
I lived in peaceful thought with all,
Ere came this proud usurper's thrall.
Why must the Emperor's grasping hand,
Oppress this once rejoicing land,

And bring a happy race to shame,
Who hold a birthright in their name?"

" Long have I proved thee, friendly bow ;
With thee the prowling wolf laid low ;
But now a crowning shot I claim—
Ne'er hung so much upon thy aim.
Among the shafts shall two be known,
That whizzing from thy string have flown.
I shudder yet to think of one,
That threatened sore my darling son.
And this a fellow shot shall be,
For country, home and liberty ! "

" Make way ! Lord Gessler comes, make way !"
  Thus broke an eager cry,
And armed as for a sudden fray,
  An archer speeded by :
Erect he held the pointed lance,
And looked around with threatening glance.

Then came a peasant woman there,
Her look depressed by grief and care ;
Her eyes with weary weeping red ;
Two children by the hand she led ;
Not theirs the joy that childhood brings,
Sorrow had checked its tender springs.

Ah ! truly had she cause to weep,
  And still for pity pray ;
For in a dungeon dark and deep,
  Her husband lingering lay.
Long months endured of sad suspense—
An honest tongue his sole offence.
They whom his labour did sustain,
Now left to misery and pain.

The archer passed, and in the rear,
Was Gessler seen approaching near
While to the captain at his side,
He talked in all his wonted pride.
He said, "Shall such a paltry land,
Thus resolute against us stand?
By Heaven! I'll curb the people still,
And force them to the Emperor's will.
Nought care I for the rights they claim,
With rebels but an idle name."

E'en as he spake, the woman moved,
   And with her children knelt;
And with her piteous prayer essayed
   Lord Gessler's heart to melt.
"Be merciful! dread Lord," her plea,
"And give my husband back to me;
My children pining cry for bread,
And bitter tears we long have shed."

"Whence this intrusion?" Gessler cried;
"Ho! wretched woman, stand aside.
Must I be vexed with childish tears;
Or list a woman's whining fears."

"Mercy! Lord Gessler we implore;
My husband unto us restore."

"Peace, woman! once more stand aside,
Lest I in anger o'er thee ride."
Regardless of the suppliant's need,
The Governor spurred his restive steed—
When, instant as a flash of light,
An arrow whizzed in rapid flight,
Clove cruel Gessler's broidered vest,
And deeply pierced his haughty breast;
And shrinking with the deadly pain,
His hands forsook the bridle rein;

Down from the horse's back he sank,
And fell upon the sloping bank :
Fast trickling from the sudden wound
His blood streamed redly o'er the ground.
In vain the captain stooping low,
Essayed to staunch the fatal flow.

Then strove that once proud Lord to speak,
Though fading eye, and pallid cheek,
And failing breath, and accents weak,
   His agony betrayed ;
The captain kneeling at his side,
To calm his troubled temper tried,
All soothing offices supplied,
   And lent him ready aid :
" May Heaven have mercy !"—Gessler said,
" That shaft can TELL alone have sped."

" True !" cried a voice,—" that shaft was mine,
Aimed now without command of thine."
The listeners saw with sudden fear,
TELL's form above the rock appear—
" Gessler," he cried, " thy tyranny
Hath met its doom—the land is free !"

The tyrant's dead—the land is free !
On went the shout of liberty.
It woke the sleepers in Lucerne ;
It roused the busy streets of Berne.
It shook Mount Pilate's forests grim ;
It swelled the monks of Bernard's hymn.
And on it went—the land is free !
Around the distant Genfer See ;
And onwards still with gathering swell,
From Uri's hills to Appenzell.
Afar from Freiburg's towers it rung ;
Through Basel sped from tongue to tongue.

It all the Gotthard's echoes woke,
And from the Jungfrau's top it spoke;
It thundered 'mid the Schreckhorn's rocks,
It pealed aloud from Zurich's clocks.
Where Constance overlooks her Lake,
The far-resounding summons spake.
It mingled with Schaffhausen's roar;
It leaped the Rhine from shore to shore;
And dwellers on the rushing Rhone,
Sent back its spirit-stirring tone.

Oh, may this ancient Alpine land,
Be ever great as she is grand;
Her mountain peaks for ever be,
The symbol of her liberty!

DAS LIED VON PANEVEGGIO.

Arie—" Yankee Doodle."

In Paneveggio lebt man frei ;
  Man kliffen kann und klaffen :
Da trinkt man gut, da schläft man sanft,
  Und da frisst man die Pfaffen.
    Kameraden ! stimmet ein,
    Preis't mit Chor und Solo
    Tiroler Land, Tiroler Wein,
    In lustig Travignolo !

Die Leute können Fichtenwald
  Und frische Luft anbieten,
Und zeigen je im Himmelsblau
  Die kühnen Dolomiten.
    Chor.

Gasthaus zum schönen Kerl ist da,
  Gar wenig and're Häuser :
Da wohnt in Fried ein dicker Wirth
  Viel grösser als der Kaiser.
    Chor.

Er isst nicht viel, doch trinken kann,
  Kann leeren manche Flaschen :
Ist ehrlich wie ein Edelmann,
  Hat immer Geld in Taschen.
    Chor.

Im Winter sitzt er traurig da
  Weil wilde Schnee-Stürm haufen :
Kein Fremder kommt, er hört kein Wort,
  Was kann er thun als—saufen ?
    Chor.

Wann Frühling kommt dann wacht er auf
  Und fängt er an zu singen—
Komm, Sommer, komm geschwind um mir
  Recht viele Gäst' zu bringen !
    Chor.

Die Wirthinn in die Küche steht,
  Und kocht die besten Speisen :
Das schmeckt wohl jedermann so gut,
  Ich muss Sie immer preisen.
    Chor.

Da bleibt der Herr Ingenieur,
  Durch Wälder hau't er Strassen ;
Und eben wenig als er raucht
  So wenig kann er spassen.
    Chor.

Doch ist er ein geschickter Mann,
  Thut Kirch' und Brücken bauen :
Was aber er am liebsten hat
  Ist Schönheit anzuschauen.
    Chor.

Ein' Dame kommt, ein' Künstlerinn—
  Die nicht im mind'sten prahlet :
Doch sie Berg, Wald und Wasserfall
  Hat wunderbar gemalet.
    Chor.

Noch eine—Santa Lucia,
  Die singt schön wie ein Engel ;
Ich möchte wohl dass wie ein Kind
  Sie führte mich am Gängel.
    Chor.

Da kommt ein' holde Sängerinn :
  Verschwindet all Gewitter—
Sie spielt so süss, all' Herzen fall'n
  Entzückt vor ihrer Zither.
    Chor.

Kommt ein Professor aus Trient,
  Die Wissenschaft mit Brille :
Sein' Weisheit aber flüchtig wird
  Wenn er gehört die Trille.
    Chor.

Und kommt der jung' Luigi da
  Sein Tanzelei zu würzen ;
Er freiet eine Sängerinn,
  Muss doch vom Soller stürzen.
    Chor.

Dann steht der Herr Skultore auf :
  Seid still, sagt er, ihr Leute !
Was hilft Gesang und Malerei ?
  In Marmor Ich arbeite !
    Chor.

Bravo ! ruft dann der Englischmann
  Hier gibt es viel zu frommen :
Zu solchen Freunden sage Ich
  In England seid willkommen !
    Kameraden ! stimmet ein,
    Preis't mit Chor und Solo
    Tiroler Land, Tiroler Wein,
    In lustig Travignolo !

SPECKBACHER AND HIS LITTLE SON.

Speckbacher und sein Söhnlein.

"Oh, take me with thee, father! the strength and hardihood
 Of men I feel, and I can dare ; nor will I spare my blood."
"Dear child, 'tis earnest yonder ; no gladsome boyish jar ;
'Tis death that lights their priming, and hearts the targets
 are."

"I have a heart within my breast, how shall I keep it right,
If I must like a coward hide, and shun the bullet's flight?"
"Remain, boy, if thou lov'st me! when thou art once a man,
Then show that thou canst do and dare, as now thy father
 can!"

Speckbacher spoke, and lifted the dear one from his breast;
But he quenched not with weeping the battle's eager zest.
Speckbacher, as the chamois, flies over stock and stone—
His darling as the chamois steals after him alone.

And soon beneath the giant feet of wondrous glacier lands,
Amid the tried and trusty few the glowing hero stands ;
And, panting in the bushes, where he his way had won,
Lurks with undaunted courage his selfsame-hearted son.

Then comes the storm of bullets and back the answer flies,
And storm on storm succeeds, and quick the mountain
 storm replies :
It is as if from rock to rock all thro' the fatal game,
Flashed serpent-like, in fiery coil, a quivering belt of flame.

But still the foemen firing, pour in their shot like hail,
And in the troop upon the heights the lead begins to fail :

The eager boy has thought thereon, and while the shower
  falls,
He running lightly here and there has gathered up the balls.

Their need is scarcely spoken, than quickly forth he springs,
And tells half shy how he had wrought, and what the store
  he brings—
How when the hostile bullets fell, he, hastening round about,
With ready hand, before they cooled, had plucked them
  quickly out.

The father took the bullets, and felt his bosom throb,
And while he loads, can scarce repress the thrilling tearful
  sob.
He would embrace, and yet must fire,—would blame yet
  must advise ;
And standing there before his boy, loud to his comrades
  cries,—

" Tyroler brothers, hearken ! this time be none ill-sped ;
The foe in murderous onset hath wasted here his lead :
Now every shot must hit the mark, whatever else befall,
For loyalty hath brought the charge, and innocence the
  ball."

A WEDDING-BREAKFAST SPEECH.

(Married—Ada Snowdon to William White.)

In old times the fairies played wonderful tricks,
Changed maidens to vixens, and men into sticks:
The sticks still survive, as in pulpits we see;
But that vixens are dead, married men all agree.
One Fairy named Hymen still lives and he plays
Such tricks as would fill his old friends with amaze:
Changes Frost into Summer, and Flint into Steel,
And Hardy to Coward, and Wolfe into Veal.
But his latest achievements all others surpass,
As you will believe when you hear of the lass
Who always was Snowdon by night and by day,
Yet never turned white, did not even look gray;
But Hymen has touched her, and, wonderful sight!
Though no longer Snowdon, she always is White.

www.ingramcontent.com/pod-product-compliance
Lightning Source LLC
Chambersburg PA
CBHW020830190426
43197CB00037B/1247